D0481782

A Book
of Days in
American History

A Book
of Days in
American History

Larry Shapiro

Charles Scribner's Sons
New York

Frontispiece
"Original Air Balloon," an English
cartoon published in 1783, shows the
balloon America, with George Washington at left in the basket, released
from English bonds after Benjamin
Franklin, wearing dark glasses, has
cut the ropes with a knife inscribed
"Sedition." Interested bystanders include France, second from left, and
Holland, right. (The Print Collection,
Lewis Walpole Library, Yale University)

Editorial Director: Maron L. Waxman

Art Direction and Design: Christopher Holme

Picture Editor: Joan P. Kerr

Editors: Hilary "Tex" Sterne, Dorian Hastings, Ann Finlayson,
    Margo Gillespie

Researchers: Alice Peck, Jonathan Crawford, Meredith Davis,
    Veronica Cruz

Special thanks to Janet Doyle, Diane Cassone, and Arnold Gopen
    for advice and assistance in preparing the illustrations and to
    Lorraine Shanley for proposing the project.

Library of Congress Cataloging-in-Publication Data
Shapiro, Larry.
    A book of days in American history.

    Includes index.
    1. United States—History—Chronology.
2. Calendars—United States.   I. Title.
E174.5.S53   1987   973'.02'02   87-4806
ISBN 0-684-18894-5

A Book
of Days in
American History

January

JANUARY 1 *(Opening illustration)*
New Americans on Ellis Island await a ferry that will take them to Manhattan. (Library of Congress)

JANUARY 3
"Its most conspicuous feature—the great towers—" Roebling proclaimed, "will be entitled to be ranked as national monuments." (Culver Pictures)

✦ 1 ✦

1673 Regular mail delivery begins between New York and Boston but will be suspended when the Dutch recapture New York later in the year. **1863** After long deliberation President Lincoln issues the Emancipation Proclamation, which grants freedom to slaves living in states that joined the rebellion. Thomas Wentworth Higginson, a New Englander then in South Carolina leading a black regiment, wrote that when an American flag was unfurled at a meeting held to announce the proclamation, "there suddenly arose a strong male voice (but rather cracked and elderly), into which two women's voices instantly blended, singing, as if by an impulse that could no more be repressed than the morning note of the song-sparrow— 'My Country, 'tis of thee, Sweet Land of Liberty, of thee I sing!'" **1892** A processing center for arriving immigrants opens on Ellis Island in New York harbor.

✦ 2 ✦

1788 Georgia ratifies the Constitution and becomes the fourth state of the Union. **1800** The free black community of Philadelphia petitions Congress to abolish slavery. Representative

John Rutledge, Jr., of South Carolina denounces the petition as a result of "this new-fangled French philosophy of liberty and equality," and the measure is put aside to expire in committee. **1882** As a way around antimonopoly laws, John D. Rockefeller's Standard Oil Company of Ohio, which controls over 90 percent of the nation's oil production, is organized as a trust in which Rockefeller will serve as "trustee" of the stock.

✦ **3** ✦

1777 General Washington reaches Princeton, New Jersey, after slipping out of Trenton the night before (and leaving behind men digging trenches to confuse General Cornwallis). At the battle of Princeton Washington's weary troops defeat two British regiments, then head for winter camp in New Brunswick. **1825** Scottish industrialist Robert Owen buys 30,000 acres in Indiana as the site of a utopian community called New Harmony. After three quarrelsome years Owen withdraws his support, having spent much of his fortune on the experiment. **1870** Ground is broken for the Brooklyn Bridge, which engineer John Roebling promises will be "the great engineering work of this Continent and of the age." **1959** Alaska is admitted to the Union as the forty-ninth state.

✦ **4** ✦

1821 An annual feast day marks the death on this day of Elizabeth Ann Seton, the first native-born U.S. Roman Catholic saint, a convert who established the nation's first parochial schools and founded the American Sisters of Charity of St. Joseph, the nation's first religious order for women. **1896** Utah is admitted to the Union as the forty-fifth state. **1904** In *Gonzalez v. Williams* the Supreme Court rules that Puerto Rican residents are not aliens and cannot be refused admission to the United States (not until 1917 will full citizenship be extended). **1923** French psychologist Emil Coué brings his self-esteem therapy to America, its centerpiece the motto "Every day in every way I am getting better and better." **1965** President Lyndon Johnson's State of the Union address calls for the creation of the Great Society, the most ambitious program of social legislation since the New Deal.

✦ 5 ✦

1836 Congressman and frontier hero Davy Crockett arrives in Texas after losing an election in Tennessee: "I told the people of my District that, if they saw fit to reelect me, I would serve them as faithfully as I had done; but if not, they might go to hell, and I would go to Texas . . . and here I am." In a few weeks he will join the forces at the Alamo. **1914** In an unprecedented confirmation of the cost advantages of standardized mass production, the Ford Motor Company adjusts its wage rates from $2.40 a day for a nine-hour day to $5.00 for an eight-hour day. **1925** Nellie Taylor Ross is inaugurated as governor of Wyoming, the first woman to hold the office. Miriam (Ma) Ferguson was elected governor of Texas in the same election but was not inaugurated until January 20. **1968** A grand jury in Boston indicts Dr. Benjamin Spock, the celebrated author of *Child and Baby Care* and elder statesman of the Vietnam War protest movement, on charges of conspiring to abet violations of the draft laws.

✦ 6 ✦

1818 General Andrew Jackson writes to President Monroe offering to launch a military campaign to seize Spanish possessions in Florida: "Let it be signified to me through any channel . . . that the possession of the Floridas would be desirable to the United States and in sixty days it will be accomplished." The president did not reply, which Jackson interpreted as a sign of approval, and in the spring he marched into St. Marks and Pensacola. **1912** New Mexico is admitted to the Union as the forty-seventh state. **1941** President Franklin D. Roosevelt's State of the Union message, dwelling on "four freedoms" imperiled by fascism, strongly declares U.S. interest in the war in Europe.

✦ 7 ✦

1784 David Landreth of Philadelphia establishes the first seed supply business in the United States. **1800** Millard Fillmore, thirteenth president of the United States, is born in Locke, New York. Fillmore, who became president upon the death of Zachary Taylor, was not renominated by his Whig party and ran unsuccessfully as a candidate of the anti-Catholic and anti-immigrant Know-Nothing party. **1896** Fannie Farmer publishes the first edition of her *Boston Cooking School Cook Book.* **1955** Marian Anderson, playing Ulrica in Verdi's *A Masked Ball,* becomes the first black singer to perform at the Metropolitan Opera in New York.

JANUARY 6

This engraving of the Battle of New Orleans by one of Andrew Jackson's engineers shows the British advancing along the canal while the Americans wait in trenches. The large house to the left is Jackson's headquarters. (Irving S. Olds Collection, New-York Historical Society)

BOSTON MEASURING SPOONS

(Four in the set)
Correct measures for

Quarter Teaspoon
Half Teaspoon
Teaspoon
Tablespoon

Made of Aluminum

Used and endorsed by highest authorities in the art of Cooking.
A necessity for careful cooks.
A delight to chafing-dish users.
Assures perfect results.
Set of four spoons postpaid, 50c.

JOHN FORD CO.
P.O. Box 1575, Boston

JANUARY 7

The Boston Cooking School emphasized exact measurements, creating a need for new kitchen implements, among them measuring spoons. (Laura Shapiro)

✦ 8 ✦

1798 The Eleventh Amendment is added to the Constitution, declaring that the federal government has no power to interfere in suits brought against a state by residents of another state. The amendment was drawn up after two South Carolina merchants were allowed to sue the state of Georgia in the U.S. Supreme Court. **1815** General Andrew Jackson fends off a British attack in the Battle of New Orleans, the last major battle of the War of 1812. Neither side is aware that a peace treaty was signed in Europe two weeks earlier. **1918** President Woodrow Wilson presents his Fourteen Points speech. Outlining an equitable resolution to World War I, it became a pillar of Allied propaganda, with hundreds of thousands of copies dropped from the air over Germany, and later served as the basis for Wilson's position at the Paris Peace Conference.

JANUARY 6
A postage stamp commemorates the
four freedoms. (U.S. Postal Service)

✦ 9 ✦

1793 George Washington is among the spectators in Philadelphia when Jean Pierre Blanchard and a dog lift off in a balloon to a height of 5,800 feet and travel fifteen miles in forty-six minutes. **1788** Connecticut ratifies the Constitution and becomes the fifth state of the Union. **1789** Former Revolutionary War general Arthur St. Clair, first governor of the Northwest Territory in what will become Ohio, signs a treaty with the Ohio Indians, whom he is trying to subdue to make the frontier more attractive to white settlers. **1913** Richard M. Nixon, thirty-seventh president, is born in Yorba Linda, California, where his father has a lemon farm.

JANUARY 9
Balloonist Blanchard carried an American flag and a U.S. passport presented to him by President Washington. (American Antiquarian Society)

✦ 10 ✦

1776 In Philadelphia British firebrand Thomas Paine publishes his pamphlet *Common Sense,* which argues that it is only common sense for the Americans to break their ties with Britain. **1901** Oil is discovered at the Spindletop field in Beaumont, Texas, which becomes the most productive in American history—148,000 barrels a day at its peak. **1920** The League of Nations is established in Geneva, largely at the instigation of President Woodrow Wilson, but the U.S. Senate, reflecting a new mood of isolationism, eventually refuses to endorse United States membership.

✦ 11 ✦

1775 Francis Salvador, a plantation owner in rural South Carolina, is elected to the colony's Provincial Congress, becoming the first Jew to hold elective office in America. In the summer of 1776, Salvador was killed in a skirmish between Revolutionaries and Cherokees loyal to the British. **1803** James Monroe and Robert R. Livingston sail for Paris to purchase the city of New Orleans. Instead, they will strike a deal for the entire Louisiana Territory—half a billion acres at less than 3 cents an acre.

JANUARY 9
Thomas Paine by John Wesley Jarvis, circa 1806. (National Gallery of Art, Washington. Gift of Marian B. Maurice)

JANUARY 12

Jacob Riis' photographs of slum dwellers and homeless children presented the perils of city life with unprecedented realism. (Riis Collection, Museum of the City of New York)

1747 The *New York Gazette* announces a lottery to raise funds to establish King's College, which will open in 1754, close during the Revolution, and reopen in 1784 as Columbia University. **1812** The steamboat *New Orleans* reaches the city of New Orleans carrying cotton from Natchez, the first cargo to come down the river by steam. The boat then begins weekly trips, with an average up-current speed of three miles per hour. **1839** In the town of Mauch Chunk, Pennsylvania, anthracite coal is used for the first time to smelt iron. **1894** Danish immigrant Jacob Riis, a crime reporter who became a crusader for New York's unemployed and working classes, gives a public lecture titled "The Need of Playgrounds and Open Spaces." **1964** U.S. Surgeon General Luther Terry describes cigarette smoking as a health hazard.

✦ 13 ✦

1733 Georgia, last of the thirteen original colonies, is established when the colony's proprietor, social reformer James Edward Oglethorpe, arrives in America bearing his charter and leading 130 settlers. Laws for the colony forbid brandy, rum, and slaves, but rum is permitted in 1742, and slavery adopted in 1749. **1794** Congress adds two stars and two stripes to the American flag to represent the newly added states of Vermont and Kentucky. **1942** German U-boats begin a harassment campaign called Operation Drum Roll against ships on the east coast, where security is casual in spite of a state of war.

✦ 14 ✦

1699 The Massachusetts Bay Colony holds a day of fasting and repentance for having wrongly condemned and punished people for practicing witchcraft: We "were for want of knowledge in our selves, and better Information from others, prevailed with to take up with such Evidence against the Accused, as on further consideration, and better Information, we justly fear was insufficient for touching the Lives of any." **1784** The Continental Congress ratifies the Treaty of Paris, formally ending the American Revolution almost three years after the fighting stopped and the British withdrew. **1799** Inventor and manufacturer Eli Whitney receives a government contract for 10,000 muskets with interchangeable parts.

JANUARY 15

Thomas Nast's *A Live Ass Kicking a Dead Lion,* which appeared in print on January 15, 1870, helped popularize the donkey as a symbol of the Democratic Party. The lion in this picture is deceased Secretary of War Stanton. Later Nast added the Republican elephant to his menagerie. (Culver Pictures)

JANUARY 15
George Catlin's painting shows Sieur
de la Salle greeting Indians near the
site of Fort Crèvecoeur. (American
Museum of Natural History)

✦ 15 ✦

1680 French explorer Sieur de la Salle, journeying down the Illinois River in hope of eventually reaching the mouth of the Mississippi, pauses at Lake Peoria to build Fort Crèvecoeur. **1831** The first American-built locomotive to pull a passenger train, Best Friend, runs from Charleston to Hamburg, South Carolina.

✦ 16 ✦

1787 Thomas Jefferson writes to Colonel Edward Carrington: "Were it left to me to decide whether we should have a government without newspapers, or newspapers without a government, I should not hesitate a moment to prefer the latter." **1883** Moved to action by a crazed office seeker's assassination of President Garfield, Congress attacks the old and corrupt system of awarding government jobs by passing the Pendleton Act, which creates the Civil Service Commission to award jobs on merit. **1897** John Dewey's essay "My Pedagogic Creed" appears in *School Journal* and is hailed as a definitive statement of the ideals of progressive education. **1920** The Eighteenth Amendment goes into effect, making it illegal to manufacture, transport, or sell alcoholic beverages in the United States.

JANUARY 16
Prohibition agents dispose of the forbidden beverage. (UPI/Bettmann Newsphotos)

✦ 17 ✦

1821 Moses Austin of Missouri receives permission from the government of Mexico to settle 300 American families in Texas. **1893** With the help of U.S. Minister John L. Stevens, American-descended planters in Honolulu overthrow the regime of Queen Liliuokalani, who appeals to the government in Washington for help in restoring her throne. **1918** Harry Garfield, the head of the wartime Fuel Administration and son of the assassinated president, causes a furor when he orders a four-day shutdown of all factories east of the Mississippi to speed coal deliveries to eastern ports in support of the war effort.

✦ 18 ✦

1830 Senator Thomas Hart Benton of Missouri, who once fired two shots at Andrew Jackson during a street fight in Nashville but later became his protégé, makes a speech in which he accuses Northeastern politicians of trying to slow development of the American West. **1854** William Walker, a notorious "filibuster," as adventurers against countries with which the United States was at peace were called, proclaims himself president of a new republic, Sonora, composed of the Mexican states of Sonora and Baja California. **1943** To save labor and steel cutting machinery for the war effort, commercial bakeries are ordered to cease the sale of sliced bread.

✦ 19 ✦

1633 Thomas Morton, twice deported from Massachusetts for hosting licentious maypole celebrations at his Indian trading post called Merry Mount, attempts in London to have the Bay

JANUARY 17

American interest in the Sandwich Islands had been on the rise since the discovery of bowhead whales in the Arctic, and by the 1850s Honolulu was said to resemble a New England whaling port; below, Queen Liliuokalani. (Library of Congress; below, UPI/Bettmann Newsphotos)

Colony's charter revoked. **1840** Lieutenant Charles Wilkes, who is leading a survey of the South Seas and polar regions on America's first maritime scientific expedition, sights Antarctica and claims it as a United States possession. Some of the 180 nautical charts produced by the expedition will be used during World War II, but Wilkes's tyrannical behavior on the three-year voyage leads to a court-martial when he returns. He is said to have been a model for Captain Ahab in Melville's *Moby Dick*. **1977** President Gerald Ford pardons Iva Toguri D'Aquino, "Tokyo Rose," who had been convicted of treason for her radio broadcasts during World War II.

✦ 20 ✦

1801 John Marshall is appointed Chief Justice of the Supreme Court. In his thirty-four years on the court, Marshall will write crucial opinions that define the power of federal courts to declare laws unconstitutional (*Marbury* v. *Madison*) and the supremacy of federal courts in cases involving conflict between the federal government and the states (*McCullough* v. *Maryland*). **1832** In a debate in the Virginia legislature, the state's small farmers argue that the plantation system based on slavery is a threat to their way of life. **1887** The government leases Pearl Harbor from Hawaii for use as a naval port. **1892** Using peach baskets in a YMCA gym, students in Springfield, Massachusetts, are introduced to the new game of basketball invented by Canadian-born Dr. James Naismith.

JANUARY 19
The Wilkes Expedition in Antarctica, painted by expedition member Titian Ramsay Peale. (Yale Collection of Western Americana, Beinecke Library)

✦ 21 ✦

1789 Publication is announced for *The Power of Sympathy; or, The Triumph of Nature,* an epistolary romance by William Hill Brown intended to "Expose the dangerous Consequences of Seduction." It is considered the first American novel. **1855** George Templeton Strong, a close observer of fellow upper class New Yorkers, notes in his diary that "there has been vast improvement during the last three or four years in the dealings of our 'upper class' with the poor; not merely in the comparative abundance of their bounty, but in the fact that it has become fashionable and creditable and not unusual for people to busy themselves in personal labors for the very poor and in personal intercourse with them. It is a very significant thing and would have been held a marvel ten years ago . . ." **1977** President Jimmy Carter offers a pardon to most Vietnam-era draft resisters.

JANUARY 24
John Sutter's adobe style fort, painted in 1849 by miner John Hovey. (Huntington Library, San Marino, California)

✦ 22 ✦

1690 At Onondaga, New York, the Iroquois tribes renew their allegiance to the British in the conflict with France. During the American Revolution, the Iroquois try to stay neutral, and Chief Cawconcaucawheteda tells the British: "You say their Powder is rotten—We have found it good. You say they are all mad, foolish, wicked and deceitful—I say you are so and they are wise for you want us to destroy ourselves in your War and they advise us to live in Peace. Their advice we intend to follow." **1944** American troops invading Italy establish a beachhead at Anzio, thirty miles south of Rome. Initial casualties are light, but a German counterthrust stalls the Allied advance toward Rome.

✦ 23 ✦

1789 Georgetown, the first Catholic college in the United States, is founded by Father John Carroll, who later becomes the first Catholic bishop in the United States. **1849** Elizabeth Blackwell graduates at the head of her class and becomes the first woman in the United States to receive a medical degree. She had been admitted to the twenty-ninth school to which she applied—Geneva College in New York, later part of Syracuse University—after the students were polled on her admission, and she had to fight for permission to attend classes in anatomy. **1862** Agoston Haraszthy, who planted the first large vineyard in the Sonoma Valley, California, receives a load of 100,000 vines representing 1400 varieties of European grapes.

✦ 24 ✦

1639 Colonists in the Connecticut settlements of Hartford, Windsor, and Wethersfield adopt the Fundamental Orders, a framework of government considered to be the first constitution in the New World. **1842** Former President John Quincy Adams, happier as a gadfly member of the House of Representatives than he had been in the White House, submits a petition on behalf of antislavery constituents in Massachusetts, who believe the time has come to begin a peaceful dissolution of the Union. **1848** Nine days before California is due to become part of the United States, a carpenter named James Wilson Marshall finds glittering particles in the refuse water where he is building a sawmill near Sacramento for John Sutter and declares, "Boys, I believe I have found a gold mine!"

JANUARY 23
"The idea of winning a doctor's degree gradually assumed the aspect of a great moral struggle," wrote Elizabeth Blackwell. (Schlesinger Library, Radcliffe College)

✦ 25 ✦

1787 Daniel Shays, leading a rebellion of debt-ridden farmers in western Massachusetts, readies his followers for an attack on the arsenal at Springfield. His 1,200 men will be routed in bitter cold the next day, but men of property fear that Shays's rebellion will not be an isolated event. The uprising is on the minds of the delegates who gather in Philadelphia in May 1787 for the Constitutional Convention. **1945** Grand Rapids, Michigan, becomes the first American city to add fluoride to its drinking water. **1961** Newly inaugurated President John F. Kennedy holds the first presidential news conference before live television cameras.

✦ 26 ✦

1787 Benjamin Franklin writes to Sarah Bache, his daughter, about the national symbol: "I wish the Bald Eagle had not been chosen as the Representative of our Country; he is a Bird of bad moral Character; like those among Men who live by Sharping and Robbing, he is generally poor, and often very lousy. The Turkey is a much more respectable Bird, and withal a true original Native of America." **1837** Michigan is admitted to the Union as the twenty-sixth state. **1838** Tennessee passes a law forbidding the sale of alcohol in taverns or stores—the first state temperance law. **1918** To deal with wartime shortages, food administrator Herbert Hoover issues a nationwide call for "wheatless" and "meatless" days. Stressing voluntary measures, Hoover had previously sent workers door-to-door with pledge cards.

✦ 27 ✦

1750 Wilderness scout Christopher Gist, exploring the Ohio territory on behalf of Eastern land speculators, records in his journal: "This night it snowed and in the morning the snow was six or seven inches deep, the wild rye appeared very green and flourishing through it and our horse had a fine feeding." Wild rye was thought to be confined to the sandy soil of New England, where by 1700 it was the second largest crop after corn. **1785** The nation's first state university, the University of Georgia, is chartered in Athens. **1888** The National Geographic Society is organized in Washington, D.C.

✦ 28 ✦

1782 Congress provides a law and funding for the use of a Great Seal, although none had yet been designed. **1878** In New Haven, Connecticut, the first commercial telephone switchboard begins service to the city's twenty-one subscribers. **1915** An act of Congress combines the Lifesaving Service and the Revenue Cutter Service to create the U.S. Coast Guard. **1916** President Woodrow Wilson nominates Louis D. Brandeis to the Supreme Court. Brandeis, renowned for his defense of the underdog and the first Jew to be appointed to the Court, is a controversial choice, and he faces stormy confirmation hearings. **1945** Led by General "Vinegar Joe" Stilwell, a truck convoy from India crosses the Burma-Chinese border, opening the Burma Road for the first time since it was seized by the Japanese.

JANUARY 28

The Brandeis appointment: "CHORUS OF GRIEF-STRICKEN CONSERVATIVES: Oh, what an associate for a pure and innocent girl! And we have tried to bring her up so carefully, too!" (Library of Congress)

✦ 29 ✦

1834 In the first use of federal troops to put down a labor dispute, President Jackson calls on the War Department to quell a "riotous assembly" of Irish workers on the Chesapeake & Ohio Railroad. **1843** William McKinley, twenty-fifth president of the United States, is born in Niles, Ohio, the son of an iron worker. **1861** Kansas becomes the thirty-fourth state of the Union, with a constitution that outlaws slavery. **1936** The Baseball Hall of Fame in Cooperstown, New York, elects its first five players: Ty Cobb, Walter Johnson, Christy Mathewson, Babe Ruth, and Honus Wagner.

✦ 30 ✦

1787 Thomas Jefferson, hearing reports of Shays's Rebellion earlier in the month, sends off a characteristically provocative opinion to the conservative James Madison: "I hold it, that a little rebellion now and then, is a good thing, and as necessary in the political world as storms in the physical." **1835** As President Andrew Jackson leaves the House of Representatives, a man fires two shots at him and misses. It is the first attempt on the life of a president. **1882** Franklin Delano Roosevelt, thirty-second president of the United States, is born in Hyde Park, New York, on an estate that his family has owned for one hundred years.

JANUARY 30

The attempt on the life of Andrew Jackson, supposedly drawn by a witness. (Culver Pictures)

BABE RUTH

CHRISTY MATHEWSON

TY COBB

ONUS WAGNER

WALTER JOHNSON

JANUARY 29
The original members of the National Baseball Hall of Fame. (All photos, National Baseball Library, Cooperstown, New York)

✦ 31 ✦

1917 The German Ambassador to the United States, Johann von Bernstorff, notifies Secretary of State Lansing that beginning the next day German submarines would attack without warning all merchant ships approaching Britain or France, including those of the neutral United States. **1958** A 30.8-pound satellite called *Explorer One,* powered by a four-stage Jupiter rocket, becomes the first American satellite to be successfully launched into orbit around the earth.

February

✦ 1 ✦

1865 While the states open hearings to ratify the Thirteenth Amendment banning slavery, General Sherman's army begins its march through South Carolina. Seventeen days later, in the worst atrocity of the campaign, his troops burn Columbia, the state capital, of no military value. **1898** The Travelers Insurance Company issues the first automobile insurance coverage. The policy indemnifies a Buffalo resident against suits brought by owners of horses. **1960** The civil rights movement begins a new phase when four black college freshmen sit down at a whites-only lunch counter at Woolworth's in Greensboro, North Carolina, and refuse to leave when denied service.

✦ 2 ✦

1811 Russian settlers establish Fort Ross, north of San Francisco, as a trading post for sea otter furs. **1869** James Oliver improves on John Deere's round blade plow by inventing a removable tempered steel blade that can withstand the temperature extremes faced by prairie homesteaders. **1912** New York's palatial passenger train station, Grand Central Terminal, opens in the center of Manhattan. **1925** Dogsled teams reach Nome, Alaska, after a 650-mile trip from Nenana, near Fairbanks, with emergency supplies of serum to fight a diphtheria epidemic. **1942** The last wartime automobile comes off the assembly line as manufacturers switch to war production.

FEBRUARY 28 *(Opening illustration)*
San Francisco in 1849, with a tent city on Telegraph Hill. (Wells Fargo Archives, San Francisco)

FEBRUARY 2
The vast interior of Grand Central Terminal, in the Beaux-Arts style popularized by Chicago's World Columbian Exposition of 1893. (Collections of the Municipal Archives of the City of New York)

FEBRUARY 1

"The whole army is burning with an insatiable desire to wreak vengeance upon South Carolina," wrote Sherman to Henry Halleck. (Library of Congress)

✦ 3 ✦

1743 To cope with the numbers of immigrants, especially indentured servants, arriving in poor health after enduring horrendous conditions aboard ships, Philadelphia establishes a pesthouse, or quarantine station for people with contagious diseases, on Fisher's Island. **1866** In the Lynn, Massachusetts, *Reporter,* a brief article describes an apparently fatal fall suffered by Mary Patterson. Mrs. Patterson, better known to posterity as Mary Baker Eddy, recovered from her injury the next day, after she opened a Bible and her eye fell on the story of Jesus healing a palsied man. From that experience she elaborated the principles of Christian Science.

✦ 4 ✦

1854 In Ripon, Wisconsin, lawyer Alvan Bovay proposes the name "Republican Party" for a new political party being organized to fight the spread of slavery. **1865** With the South's defeat a virtual certainty, Robert E. Lee exchanges his former title—General of the Army of Northern Virginia—for a new one: Confederate General in Chief. This has been proposed by Virginia's General Assembly, in a last-ditch attempt to "inspire increased confidence in the final success of our arms." **1887** The Interstate Commerce Act is signed into law, setting up a commission to regulate rates on the railroads and ensure that the interests of farmers and small businessmen are represented. **1932** Lake Placid, New York, hosts the first winter Olympic Games.

✦ 5 ✦

1736 The British pioneers of Methodism, John and Charles Wesley, arrive in Savannah, Georgia. Their American mission fares poorly, but the Wesleys' eloquent disciple, George Whitefield, carries on their work. **1864** President Lincoln writes to War Secretary Stanton about a proposed loyalty oath: "On principle, I dislike an oath which requires a man to swear he *has* not done wrong. . . . I think it is enough if the man does no wrong *hereafter*." **1972** After numerous hijacking incidents, United States airlines begin mandatory inspection of passengers and luggage.

✦ 6 ✦

1778 The United States signs a treaty of military alliance with France to "maintain effectually the liberty, Sovereignty, and independence" of the United States. France gives its consent to an American conquest of Canada and Bermuda, and the United States agrees to be France's ally in any war with Britain. The next military treaty the United States enters into is the NATO pact, in 1949. **1788** Massachusetts ratifies the Constitution and becomes the sixth state of the Union. **1816** John Stevens of Hoboken, New Jersey, is granted the first charter to build a railroad in the United States. **1820** Eighty-six free blacks sail out of New York harbor aboard the *Mayflower of Liberia*. Their destination is Sierra Leone, a British colony that welcomes free blacks and fugitive slaves.

✦ 7 ✦

1827 America's first ballet company has its debut at the Bowery Theater in New York. **1839** Henry Clay, patriarch of the Whig Party, tries to build his presidential prospects by opposing slavery while also denouncing abolition, but declares in a Senate speech, "I had rather be right than president." **1886** Federal troops are called into Seattle to quell rioting against Chinese immigrants that leaves 400 people homeless.

✦ 8 ✦

1735 Colley Cibber's *Flora; or, The Hob in the Well,* the first opera performed in the colonies, is staged in Charleston, South Carolina. **1861** Elizabeth Cady Stanton pleads unsuccessfully at a special session of the New York State Senate to make willful desertion and cruelty grounds for divorce (this would not become New York law until 1966). **1887** Congress passes the Dawes Act, which offers citizenship and land to any male Indian "who has voluntarily taken up . . . his residence separate and apart from any tribe . . . and has adopted the habits of civilized life." **1894** Congress repeals one of the cornerstones of Reconstruction, the Enforcement Act, thereby making it easier for some states to disenfranchise black voters. **1910** The Boy Scouts of America, modeled after a British organization, are chartered in Washington, D.C.

FEBRUARY 7
Henry Clay in a statesmanlike pose by John Neagle. (Library of Congress)

FEBRUARY 7
Rioting against Chinese immigrants was widespread in the Far West. (Culver Pictures)

✦ 9 ✦

1773 William Henry Harrison, ninth president of the United States, is born in Berkeley, Virginia. In his 1840 campaign Harrison's log cabin image and military nickname ("Tippecanoe") were promoted aggressively through log cabin teacups, handkerchiefs, sunbonnets, Tippecanoe tobacco and shaving soap, and Old Cabin Whiskey. **1861** Jefferson Davis, former U.S. secretary of war and senator from Mississippi, is elected provisional president of the Confederate States of America. **1870** Congress establishes the U.S. Weather Bureau. **1964** The Beatles are presented to the nation on the Ed Sullivan Show.

✦ 10 ✦

1763 In the Treaty of Paris ending the French and Indian War, "half the continent . . . changed hands at the scratch of a pen" (Francis Parkman) as France surrenders its claims to Canada. **1772** The Pennsylvania *Packet and General Advertiser* advertises a reward for runaway indentured servants. **1846** The westward migration of the Mormons begins from Nauvoo, Illinois, under the leadership of Brigham Young. **1863** Alanson Crane is awarded a patent for a fire extinguisher.

✦ 11 ✦

1789 William Short, Thomas Jefferson's secretary, friend, and confidante, writes to Jefferson from Italy that he has obtained a macaroni mold, as requested. Short's return with this implement marks the debut of pasta in the United States. **1808** In Wilkes-Barre, Pennsylvania, Jesse Fell experiments with open-grate burning of anthracite, which until then had been found too hot to burn in household stoves. **1812** Governor Elbridge Gerry of Massachusetts signs a redistricting law that divides his state into politically convenient but geographically tortuous chunks—the first Gerrymandering.

✦ 12 ✦

1793 Congress enacts the first fugitive slave law, making it a crime to hide or protect a runaway slave. **1809** Abraham Lincoln, the sixteenth president of the United States, is born in a backwoods cabin near Hodgenville, Kentucky. He would later write, "It is a great piece of folly to attempt to make anything out of my early life. It can all be condensed into a single sentence and that sentence you will find in Gray's Elegy—'The short and simple annals of the poor.'" **1839** A boundary dispute between Maine and New Brunswick leads to the "Aroostook War," and although the states call up their militias and Nova Scotia and the United States appropriate war funds, the

FEBRUARY 11

Elbridge Gerry's highly political redistricting plan inspired this cartoon creature called a "Gerrymander." (American Antiquarian Society)

campaign flag for William Henry
arrison, the "log cabin and hard
der" candidate who ran on his mili-
-y record and humble origins and
us, his followers proclaimed, "OK."
Jattatuck Museum, Waterbury,
onnecticut)

violence is limited to scuffles between Maine land agents and
Canadian lumberjacks. **1909** A group of black and white leaders, including W. E. B. Du Bois and Oswald Garrison Villard,
issues a call for a militant civil rights organization to combat
growing violence against blacks. Out of this comes the National
Association for the Advancement of Colored People, or
NAACP. **1924** *Rhapsody in Blue,* George Gershwin's attempt to
create a distinctive American classical music with jazz and popular roots, receives a heavily publicized first performance by
Paul Whiteman's Orchestra.

✦ 13 ✦

1635 Classes begin at Boston Latin School, the first public school in the United States. **1741** In Philadelphia, Andrew Bradford publishes the opening issue of the first American magazine, titled *American Magazine, or A Monthly View of the Political State of the British Colonies.* **1866** The Clay County Savings Bank in Liberty, Missouri, is robbed by young Jesse James in his first bank holdup. **1886** Influential painter and photographer Thomas Eakins, who stresses anatomical realism, resigns from the Philadelphia Academy of Art after a controversy arises over his use of male nudes in a class that includes women.

✦ 14 ✦

1817 Black History Week commemorates the birth of author and lecturer Frederick Douglass, although his actual birthdate is uncertain: "I have no accurate knowledge of my age, never having seen any authentic record containing it. By far the larger part of the slaves know as little of their age as horses know of theirs, and it is the wish of most masters within my knowledge to keep their slaves thus ignorant." **1859** Oregon is admitted to the Union as the thirty-third state. **1886** The California orange groves ship the first trainload of fruit to the East. **1912** Arizona becomes the forty-eighth state in the Union. **1929** In Chicago six members of the Bugsy Moran crime gang are lined up against a garage wall and shot by a rival gang, and the St. Valentine's Day Massacre enters American folklore.

✦ 15 ✦

1493 Christopher Columbus, reporting to the Spanish court on his first voyage to the New World, says that he has "so far

FEBRUARY 14

The orange grove and vineyard of J. G. McDonald, Alameda and Washington Streets, Los Angeles, in the 1880s. (New York Public Library)

,000 REWARD.—WHO DESTROYED THE MAINE?—$50,000 REWA.

NEW YORK JOURNAL
AND ADVERTISER. FIRST EDITION.

NO. 3,572.   Copyright, 1898, by W. R. Hearst.—NEW YORK, THURSDAY, FEBRUARY 17, 1898.—16 PAGES.   PRICE ONE CENT

DESTRUCTION OF THE WAR SHIP MAINE WAS THE WORK OF AN ENEMY

$50,000!
$50,000 REWARD!
For the Detection of the Perpetrator of the Maine Outrage!

Assistant Secretary Roosevelt Convinced the Explosion of the War Ship Was Not an Accident.

The Journal Offers $50,000 Reward for the Conviction of the Criminals Who Sent 258 American Sailors to Their Death. Naval Officers Unanimous That the Ship Was Destroyed on Purpose.

$50,000!
$50,000 REWARD!
For the Detection of the Perpetrator of the Maine Outrage!

NAVAL OFFICERS THINK THE MAINE WAS DESTROYED BY A SPANISH MINE.

FEBRUARY 15

With William Randolph Hearst taking the lead in his *New York Journal,* American newspapers played up tensions and helped make war with Spain a popular cause. Another paper, Joseph Pulitzer's *World,* sent its own divers to examine the wreck of the *Maine.*

found no human monstrosities, as many expected." **1764** St. Louis is founded as a French trading post by the fur trader Pierre Laclede Ligueste. **1804** In passing a law requiring gradual emancipation, New Jersey becomes the last Northern state to abolish slavery. **1898** The American battleship *Maine* blows up in Havana harbor, killing 260 crew members. There is an immediate assumption that Spanish sabotage was responsible.

✦ 16 ✦

1804 Lieutenant Stephen Decatur strikes back at Tripoli pirates who had boarded the U.S. Navy frigate *Philadelphia* and set it ablaze. **1933** The Senate votes to repeal the Eighteenth Amendment, which begins the legal process of overturning Prohibition. **1937** A patent for the synthetic fiber nylon is awarded to the DuPont Corporation, where it was developed by chemist Wallace H. Carothers.

✦ 17 ✦

1801 After thirty-six ballots the House breaks an Electoral College tie and elects Thomas Jefferson as president and Aaron Burr as vice president. President John Adams has been defeated in his reelection attempt, but the system survives a bitter transfer of power from the Federalist to the Republican-Democrat Party. **1913** The International Exhibit of Modern Art is held at New York City's 69th Regiment Armory. For artists, for the art-loving public, and for an astonished general public, the Armory Show is an introduction to nonrepresentational, post-Impressionist styles of European painting. **1981** The Chrysler Corporation reports the largest corporate losses in American history.

✦ 18 ✦

1688 In the first formal protest against slavery in America, the monthly meeting of the Germantown, Pennsylvania, Society of Friends votes a protest against slavery, or "the traffic of menbody." **1736** Dr. William Douglass, the only physician in Boston with a medical degree, writes to a friend in New York: "We have lately in Boston formed a medical society. . . . We design from time to time to publish some short pieces." **1842** Over 200 notables gather at a banquet in New York to honor Charles Dickens, visiting from England and, at age thirty, already famous here. Many of those feting him on this day will be hurt when his impressions of America are published.

✦ 19 ✦

1803 Congress admits Ohio to the Union as the seventeenth state. With a large population of migrants from New England, Ohio is the first state in which slavery is outlawed from the start, and in time will serve as the major thoroughfare for the Underground Railroad. **1942** President Franklin Roosevelt legalizes the detention of Japanese-Americans by giving the secretary of war authority to exclude anyone who presents a security risk from specified areas. By the end of March about 110,000 Japanese residents of the West Coast have been taken from their homes and sent to internment camps, where they are held until December 17, 1944. **1945** The U.S. Marines land on Iwo Jima island, which is sought as a base for fighter planes. Initial resistance is deceptively light.

✦ 20 ✦

1950 In a six-hour speech Wisconsin's flamboyant Senator Joseph McCarthy proclaims that he has documents that identify numerous Communist agents working in the federal government. The Wisconsin Republican has made this claim frequently in recent weeks, but this occasion motivates a Senate subcommittee to begin investigating his charges. **1962** "Cape is go, and I am go" declares John Glenn as he takes off in *Friendship 7,* beginning a three-orbit flight around the earth, the first manned American orbital space flight.

FEBRUARY 20
"I have here in my hand . . . "
Herblock's cartoon shows Senator McCarthy presenting his evidence in Senate hearings.

FEBRUARY 20
Crowds in Grand Central Terminal watch John Glenn's takeoff into space. (AP/Wide World Photos)

FEBRUARY 21
Sequoya shows the Cherokee alphabet. (Library of Congress)

✦ 21 ✦

1828 The first newspaper in an Indian language, the *Cherokee Phoenix,* is published in New Echota, Georgia. It is written in an eighty-six symbol Cherokee alphabet, invented by Indian linguist Sequoya. **1885** The completed Washington Monument is dedicated almost 100 years after plans for the structure were adopted. **1902** Dr. Harvey Cushing, considered the first American surgical specialist in the brain and nervous system, undertakes his first brain operation. **1965** Black separatist leader Malcolm X, who had recently broken with his mentor, Elijah Muhammed, and expressed new faith in the possibility of racial reconciliation, is assassinated during a speech in New York.

✦ 22 ✦

1732 George Washington is born in Bridges Creek, Virginia, his father a land speculator and planter who had once been widowed, his mother an orphan with a comfortable inheritance. **1775** The American Manufactory of Woolens, Linens, and Cottons, the nation's first joint stock company, offers its shares at £10. **1819** In the Adams-Onis Treaty, signed in Washington by Secretary of State John Quincy Adams and Spanish Minister Luis de Onis, Spain cedes East Florida to the United States along the Sabine River. **1860** The workers of Lynn, Massachusetts, shoemaking center of the nation, strike for higher wages and, after successful demonstrations and favorable publicity, win their major demands. The ranks of strikers include many women.

✦ 23 ✦

1778 Baron von Steuben joins the Continental Army at Valley Forge and begins drilling General Washington's infantry in simplified military tactics. **1813** In Waltham, Massachusetts, the Boston Manufacturing Company founds the first cotton mill in which the entire process from spinning to weaving is centralized under one roof. **1850** "I wish to unite with you in every effort to encourage a taste for this style of music so cried down by opera managers," writes songwriter Stephen Foster to Ed Christy, leader of the Christy Minstrels. Foster, who received $100 for his "Oh! Susannah," but is struggling for recognition, offers Christy his new minstrel song, "De Camptown Races." **1954** Children in the Pittsburgh public schools receive the first field testing of the polio vaccine developed by Dr. Jonas Salk.

✦ 24 ✦

1868 The House of Representatives votes to impeach President Andrew Johnson of "high crimes and misdemeanors," and preparations begin for a trial unprecedented in American history. **1887** On his twenty-first birthday Winslow Homer quits his apprenticeship to a lithographer to try to go it alone as a free-lance illustrator. **1917** The British Secret Service turns over the text of the intercepted "Zimmerman telegram," revealing German plans to entice Mexico into World War I by offering it the "lost territory" of Texas, Arizona, and New Mexico as a reward. **1977** President Jimmy Carter announces that in making foreign aid contributions, his administration will be guided by the recipients' human rights record.

FEBRUARY 22
he striking Lynn shoe workers, pro-ected by city guards. (Culver Pic-ures)

Josiah Gregg's engraving *March of the Caravan:* "I have hardly known a man who has ever become familiar with the kind of life which I led for so many years, that has not relinquished it with regret." (Yale Collection of Western Americana, Beinecke Library)

✦ 25 ✦

1836 Samuel Colt patents the six shooter. **1840** Pioneer trader Josiah Gregg begins his fourth and last trek on the Santa Fe trail. Later, after his retirement, he would reflect: "Since that time I have striven in vain to reconcile myself to the even tenor of civilized life in the United States; and have sought in its amusements and its society a substitute for those high excitements which have attached me so strongly to prairie life. Yet I am almost ashamed to confess that scarcely a day passes without my experiencing a pang of regret that I am not now roving at large upon those western plains." **1866** General John Pope reports gloomily on the prospects for settling the Great Plains, telling General Sherman that the area was "beyond the reach of agriculture, and must always remain a great uninhabited desert." **1870** Hiram R. Revels, appointed to fill out the unexpired term of Jefferson Davis as Senator from Mississippi, becomes the first black to take a seat in Congress. **1901** The U.S. Steel Corporation is organized as a combine of smaller companies under the directorship of J. P. Morgan. Andrew Carnegie sells out his shares so he can devote himself to philanthropy.

✦ 26 ✦

1732 The first mass is celebrated at Philadelphia's Roman Catholic Church, the only Catholic Church built in the thirteen colonies before the Revolution. Catholics elsewhere heard mass in private homes. **1773** Construction is authorized for Philadelphia's new Walnut Street jail, conceived as a Quaker alternative to corporal punishment, where penitent prisoners (thus the word "penitentiary") could reflect on their crimes. To enhance the opportunities for reflection, individual cells were added to the large rooms typical of colonial prisons, and so the practice of solitary confinement was born.

✦ 27 ✦

1788 An incident in which free blacks had been abducted and transported to Martinique leads to a protest in Boston. Led by Revolutionary War veteran Prince Hall, founder of the first black Masonic lodge, the free blacks of Massachusetts bring their grievances to the state assembly, which finally declares slave trading illegal and offers monetary damages to kidnapping victims. **1869** Congress passes the Fifteenth Amendment, which guarantees to citizens the right to vote regardless of "race, color, or previous condition of servitude." It will become law on March 30, 1870. It does not specify that it applies only to "male inhabitants" as does the Fourteenth, but it will be administered as if it does. **1883** Oscar Hammerstein, well-known as a theater manager and opera impresario, patents the first practical cigar rolling machine.

✦ 28 ✦

1794 Swiss immigrant Albert Gallatin, the first naturalized American to have an important political career, runs into trouble with his adversaries in the Federalist Party, who bar him from his Senate seat on a technicality. **1827** The nation's first passenger railroad, the Baltimore & Ohio, is chartered by local merchants, who hope the line will compete for inland business with the burgeoning steamboat trade, which is leaving Baltimore behind because of its lack of navigable streams. **1849** The first boatload of Gold Rush hopefuls from back east arrives in San Francisco. The alcalde of Monterey reports: "The farmers have thrown aside their plows, the lawyers their briefs, the doctors their pills, the priests their prayer books, and all are now digging gold."

✦ 29 ✦

1692 In Salem, Massachusetts, Tituba, the Indian servant of the Reverend Samuel Parris, is accused of witchcraft, along with Sarah Good. **1704** The village of Deerfield, on the northwest frontier of Massachusetts, is attacked and destroyed by French and Indian warriors. Fifty residents are killed and 100 abducted and held for ransom. **1940** Hattie McDaniel becomes the first black movie star to win an Academy Award: for Best Supporting Actress in *Gone With the Wind*.

BRUARY 29

he Deerfield massacre, as illustrated
Redeemed Captive Returning to Zion,
eyewitness account by the Rever-
d John Williams, one of the pris-
ers taken in the attack.

Yellowstone National Park, Hot Springs and Geysers.
W. H. JACKSON, Photographer, Washington, D. C.

March

Dept of Interior, U. S. Geological Survey of the Territories.

Prof. F. V. HAYDEN, in charge.

37.—Upper Basins. Soda Springs, Gardiner's River.

✦ 1 ✦

1780 After a campaign by an alliance of Philadelphia blacks and white shopkeepers and artisans, Pennsylvania becomes the first state to abolish slavery. **1790** Congress authorizes the first national census. When completed in August, it shows a population of 3,929,625, including 697,624 slaves and 59,557 free blacks. Massachusetts is the only state to report no slaves. Virginia is the most populous state with 747,000 residents and Philadelphia the largest city, with a population of 42,444. The population of London at this time is close to 1 million. **1867** Nebraska becomes the thirty-seventh state of the Union. **1872** Congress creates Yellowstone National Park, the nation's first national park, but fails to appropriate money to maintain it. **1932** The nineteen-month-old son of Charles and Anne Morrow Lindbergh is kidnapped from their home in New Jersey. **1961** President Kennedy creates the Peace Corps.

✦ 2 ✦

1809 "Never did a prisoner released from his chains, feel such relief as I shall on shaking off the shakles of power," writes Thomas Jefferson, his second term as president over and the prospect of retiring to his beloved Monticello ahead. **1829** John Dix of Boston founds the New England Asylum for the Blind, America's first school for educating the blind. **1863** A track width of 4 feet 8½ inches is adopted for the Union Pacific Railroad. This will become the standard for most railroads in the world. **1887** Congress passes the Hatch Act to set up agricultural research stations. **1949** A B-52 bomber completes the world's first nonstop global flight by refueling four times in midair.

✦ 3 ✦

1820 After furious debate and passage in the House by 90 votes to 87, the Missouri Compromise becomes law with the hope that it will resolve the conflict between opponents and advocates of slavery: Missouri joins the Union as a slave state and Maine as a free state, and new slave states are prohibited in the Louisiana Purchase territory north of the 36 degrees 30 minutes north latitude. **1842** Massachusetts restricts factory workers under the age of twelve to a ten-hour workday, a forward-looking but unenforceable law. **1845** Florida is admitted to the Union as the twenty-seventh state. **1855** At the suggestion of Secretary of War Jefferson Davis, Congress appropriates $30,000 to import Egyptian camels for service in the

MARCH 1 *(Opening illustration)*
Stereograph of Yellowstone by W. H. Jackson, the first photographer of the region. (International Museum of Photography at George Eastman House)

MARCH 4
Outgoing and incoming presidents on Inauguration Day, 1933. (UPI/Bettmann Newsphotos)

MARCH 2
Construction Superintendent Samuel Reed surveys track grade. (Library of Congress)

Time Table of the Holyoke Mills,

To take effect on and after Jan. 3d, 1853.

The standard being that of the Western Rail Road, which is the Meridian time at Cambridge.

MORNING BELLS.

First Bell ring at 4.40, A. M.   Second Bell ring in at 5, A. M.

YARD GATES

Will be opened at ringing of Morning Bells, of Meal Bells, and of Evening Bells, and kept open ten minutes.

WORK COMMENCES

At ten minutes after last Morning Bell, and ten minutes after Bell which "rings in" from Meals.

BREAKFAST BELLS.

October 1st, to March 31st, inclusive, ring out at 7, A. M. ; ring in at 7.30, A. M.
April 1st, to Sept. 30th, inclusive, ring out at 6.30, A. M. ; ring in at 7, A. M.

DINNER BELLS.

Ring out at 12.30, P. M. ; ring in at 1, P. M.

EVENING BELLS.

Ring out at 6.30,* P. M.

* Excepting on Saturdays when the Sun sets previous to 6.30.   At such times, ring out at Sunset.

In all cases, the *first* stroke of the Bell is considered as marking the time.

MARCH 3
The work schedule at midcentury for the textile capital of Holyoke, Massachusetts. Since standard time zones hadn't yet been established, the time was set locally by the railroads. (M. B. Schnapper)

Southwest. Davis' plan is to fight Indians by mounting howitzers on the camels' humps, but the project fails for lack of experienced cameleers. **1871** The Indian Appropriation Act nullifies all treaties with the tribes and makes Indians wards of the federal government. **1873** Under the Comstock Act, named for antipornography crusader Anthony Comstock, it becomes illegal to send birth control information or writing judged obscene through the mail. Comstock serves as a volunteer special agent of the post office to help enforce the act.

✦ **4** ✦

1789 The Congress created under the new Constitution holds its opening session at temporary headquarters in New York City. Only nine of the twenty-two Senators were able to show up in time, and only thirteen of the fifty-nine members of the House. **1791** Vermont ends a brief existence as an independent republic and is admitted to the Union as the fourteenth state. **1933** On this day of Franklin Delano Roosevelt's inauguration, outgoing President Hoover defends his record on the Depression: "We have done all we can do; there is nothing more to be done."

MARCH 5
A contemporary—and somewhat fanciful—portrayal of the Boston Massacre. (Mansell Collection, London)

✦ 5 ✦

1770 Nine British soldiers guarding the Boston customshouse shoot at a crowd of hecklers who were armed with clubs. Five colonists are killed, and news of the "Boston Massacre" spreads quickly through the colonies. **1820** A party of missionaries from New England arrives in Hawaii and receives a welcome from the king. Honolulu's Mission House, prefabricated in Boston, follows on a whaling ship. **1923** Montana and Nevada pass the nation's first old age pension laws. Montana's coverage provides $25 monthly to residents over the age of seventy. **1933** To halt widespread withdrawals and create time to restore confidence, President Roosevelt orders the nation's banks to close for a ten-day "bank holiday."

MARCH 8
A ticket for the ill-fated Virginia lottery. (Society of Antiquaries of London)

✦ 6 ✦

1836 General Antonio Lopez Santa Ana leads 3,000 Mexican troops across the Rio Grande in a raid on the Alamo, a fortified mission in San Antonio held by 200 soldiers of the rebellious Texas republic. All the defenders are killed. **1857** The Supreme Court declares that Dred Scott, a slave, could not sue for his freedom even though he had been brought into territory where slavery was outlawed, because as a slave he was property and had no right to sue in any circumstance. The court ruling

ARCH 5
This is the happiest day in three
ears," quipped Will Rogers on the
ank closing. "We have no jobs, we
ave no money, we have no banks;
nd if Roosevelt had burned down
ne Capitol, we would have said,
'hank God, he started a fire under
omething.'" (UPI/Bettmann
ewsphotos)

also invalidates the Missouri Compromise, upsetting a delicate balance which had kept peace between free and slave states since 1820.

✦ 7 ✦

1638 Midwife Anne Hutchinson leaves Massachusetts after being excommunicated for repeated acts of heretical preaching. **1839** Painter Samuel F. B. Morse visits photography pioneer Louis Daguerre in Paris. Daguerre shows him some pictures ("No painting or engraving ever approached it," Morse would write), but refuses to explain the daguerreotype process. **1945** An advance party of the U.S. Army crosses the Rhine into Germany at Remagen, making its passage over the only bridge not blown up by the retreating Germans.

✦ 8 ✦

1622 In London the owners of the Virginia colony are forbidden by the Crown to continue financing the struggling colony through the lottery that has kept the enterprise going since 1612. By 1624 the colony has failed and falls out of private hands into direct rule of the king. **1855** The first train crosses the majestic new suspension bridge at Niagara Falls. The world's first large railroad suspension bridge is the work of immigrant German engineer John A. Roebling. **1864** Ulysses S. Grant arrives in Washington to meet President Lincoln and receive a promotion to lieutenant general, which makes him second only to the president in command of the army. It is a startling turn of fortune for Grant, who has a reputation for hard drinking, had been forced out of the army, and was at times reduced to selling firewood on street corners.

1862 The Union's ironclad ship, USS *Monitor,* arrives at Hampton Roads, Virginia, from New York to meet the challenge of the *Merrimac,* which has been wreaking havoc on the Union's wooden ships. The first battle between two ironclad battleships begins about nine in the morning and continues for two hours with little damage to the ships but many injuries to the crew members. There is no clear winner. **1892** Outraged by an incident in which she knew the victim, journalist Ida Wells-Barnett begins her investigations of lynching in the South. **1916** In an act of reprisal against the United States for permitting his rival, Venustiano Carranza, to transport troops on American railroads, rebel General Francisco "Pancho" Villa leads 1,500 of his men into New Mexico and kills 17 Americans.

✦ 10 ✦

1848 The Senate ratifies the Treaty of Guadalupe-Hidalgo, ending the war with Mexico. By the terms of the treaty Mexico gives up its claim to Texas north of the Rio Grande and accepts a $15 million payment for the transfer of California and the present sites of Nevada, Utah, and much of Arizona, New Mexico, Colorado, and Wyoming. **1876** Alexander Graham Bell, forced to start his own company because his invention had been dismissed as a toy, speaks the first words over the telephone, calling to his assistant, "Mr. Watson, come here, I want you."

MARCH 12

Crusading liberal Carl Schurz, an irresistible target for caricature. (Culver Pictures)

ARCH 9

he *Monitor* and the *Merrimac* clash.
either vessel triumphed, but the
reat of the ironclad *Merrimac* was
eutralized by this encounter. (Mabel
ady Garvan Collection, Yale Uni-
rsity Art Gallery)

✦ 11 ✦

1861 The Confederate States adopt a constitution that resembles the United States constitution in language and most of its provisions and even prohibits the African slave trade. **1941** The House passes and President Roosevelt signs the Lend-Lease Bill, which gives the president greater authority to lend military supplies without committing the United States to entering a war. The intended recipient is England, which continues to fight on almost alone against Germany and Italy. Prime Minister Winston Churchill will call Lend-Lease "the most unsordid act in the history of any nation."

✦ 12 ✦

1877 In Philadelphia, John Wanamaker opens an immense retail store in which great varieties of merchandise are organized into departments—the department store. **1877** Carl Schurz becomes the first German-born cabinet member when he joins the Hayes administration as secretary of the interior. As senator from Missouri, Schurz fought his own party's corruption during the Grant administration and broke with the Republicans until Hayes brought him back into the fold. **1912** The Girl Scouts of America are founded in Savannah, Georgia, by Juliet Low. **1933** President Roosevelt gives the first of his "fireside chats," making innovative use of the radio as a means of mass communication.

ARCH 10

rowds were astonished when Bell
xhibited the telephone—here at a
emonstration in Salem, Massachu-
tts—but Western Union was unim-
·essed, and the *New York Tribune*
ked, "Of what use is such an in-
·ntion?" (New York Public Library)

✦ 13 ✦

1687 Father Eusebio Kino begins his missionary work in the Southwest. The Italian-born, Austrian-trained Jesuit would found several Spanish missions in Arizona, help introduce the Spanish horse to the region, and conclude from his travels down the lower Colorado River that California is a peninsula, not an island. **1885** President Grover Cleveland speaks out against the incursion of white settlers into Indian territory in Oklahoma. In four years the federal government will declare the land open to white settlement. **1923** Engineer Lee De Forest, already famous as an inventor of radio, demonstrates his Phonofilm device for making movies with sound.

✦ 14 ✦

1681 King Charles II grants the Quaker merchant William Penn an immense tract of land in the colonies—Pennsylvania, it will be called—in payment for debts owed to Penn's father, an admiral who had been Oliver Cromwell's general-at-sea. **1794** New Englander Eli Whitney patents the cotton gin, a cylinder with circular saws and bristles that strip the seeds from the cotton. **1891** Congress approves the International Copyright Act, which protects foreign authors from piracy by American publishers. This had been a sore point with Charles Dickens and other European writers, who were widely read in the United States but scarcely rewarded. **1900** Encouraged by the Klondike gold strikes, Congress makes gold the standard for United States currency.

✦ 15 ✦

1767 Andrew Jackson, seventh president of the United States, is born at Careton's Pond, North Carolina. **1783** General Washington addresses the rebellious army at Newburgh, New York, and shames the soldiers out of staging a coup and naming him dictator. **1820** Maine becomes the twentieth state of the Union. **1869** The Cincinnati Red Stockings become the first openly professional baseball team, some years after under-the-table payments for playing became common. The *Lakeside Monthly* will describe the Red Stockings as "shiftless young men, debasing a fine game with their open greed." **1875** America's first cardinal of the Roman Catholic Church, John McCloskey, is invested at St. Patrick's Cathedral in New York City. **1919** Veterans of the American Expeditionary Force found the American Legion in Paris and pledge the organization to "detecting anti-American activities everywhere and seizing every opportunity to speak plainly and openly for 100 percent Americanism and for nothing else."

MARCH 16

Robert H. Goddard displays one of his rocket experiments in 1928. This one was not a success. (Clark University, Worcester, Massachusetts)

Detail of a view of West Point, by George Catlin. (West Point Museum Collections, United States Military Academy)

✦ 16 ✦

1751 James Madison, guiding light at the Constitutional Convention and fourth president of the United States, is born in Port Conway, Virginia. **1802** The Military Academy at West Point, New York, is founded as a training school for officers and engineers. **1827** The first edition appears of *Freedom's Journal,* the first newspaper published by blacks for a black audience: "Too long have others spoken for us." **1868** The impeachment trial of President Andrew Johnson ends in an acquittal. **1926** The first liquid fuel rocket, forerunner of those which will be sent above the earth's atmosphere, is launched by Robert H. Goddard in Auburn, Massachusetts.

Little Eva and Uncle Tom, from
Uncle Tom's Cabin.

✦ 17 ✦

1775 Nicholas Cresswell, an Englishman stranded in America during the Revolution, reports from Alexandria, Virginia, that he "went to a Ball made by the Irish Gentry in commemoration of St. Patrick." The nation's first public celebration of the holiday is thought to be in 1737, sponsored by Boston's Irish Charitable Society. **1811** The *New Orleans,* the first workable sidewheel steamboat, is put into the water in Pittsburgh. The builder is Nicholas Roosevelt, great-granduncle of Theodore Roosevelt.

✦ 18 ✦

1692 William Penn is deprived of his governing powers, and Pennsylvania becomes a royal colony after Pennsylvania's Quakers resisted involvement in the war against France. **1831** The Supreme Court rules that Cherokees are a "domestic dependent," in Chief Justice Marshall's words, not a foreign power, and cannot sue in federal courts. "Their relation to the United States resembles that of a ward to his guardian." **1837** Grover Cleveland, to become the twenty-second and twenty-fourth presidents, is born in Caldwell, New Jersey. He once remarked that a monument should be built for him, "not for anything I have ever done, but for the foolishness I have put a stop to."

✦ 19 ✦

1628 Ninety British merchants, most of them of the nonconformist sect known as Puritans, are granted a patent for a trading post and land in the New World; they call themselves the New England Company. In a year a successor, the Massachusetts Bay Colony, will be granted a charter to establish a colony. **1831** The first recorded bank robbery in the United States takes place in New York City, where the City Bank is opened with a set of duplicate keys and $245,000 is stolen. **1918** By act of Congress Standard Time is modified to create Daylight Saving Time, a wartime fuel-saving measure.

✦ 20 ✦

1822 William Henry Ashley advertises in the *Missouri Republican* for men to develop the fur trade at the source of the Mississippi River. Ashley's Rocky Mountain Fur Company becomes the first to do most of its own trapping rather than depend on trade with the Indians for its furs. **1852** *Uncle Tom's Cabin,* serialized in an abolitionist newspaper the year before, is published in book form, and 1 million copies are sold within six months. According to Harriet Beecher Stowe, "God wrote it. I merely wrote his dictation." **1895** Robert Deniston Hune, who had achieved almost total control over the Pacific salmon industry, backs down from his attempt to extend his empire to Alaska in exchange for an agreement by an Alaska trust to stay out of Washington.

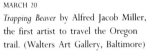

MARCH 20
Trapping Beaver by Alfred Jacob Miller, the first artist to travel the Oregon trail. (Walters Art Gallery, Baltimore)

✦ 21 ✦

1621 A final group of passengers departs the *Mayflower* after spending the winter on board, anchored off the coast of the Plymouth colony. **1868** Sorosis, America's first professional club for women, is founded in New York City. **1947** The first Republican-controlled Congress since Franklin Roosevelt's election in 1932 approves an amendment limiting presidents to two terms or ten years in office.

✦ 22 ✦

1621 A treaty is signed by Governor Carver of the Plymouth Colony and Massasoit of the Wampanoags, forming a defensive alliance. Negotiated by Squanto, who had learned English when he was captured and brought back to England in 1615, the treaty will last for fifty-four years. **1765** Parliament passes the Stamp Act, which is immediately denounced in the colonies as a revenue measure benefiting England at the expense of the colonists. The measure is repealed after London merchants complain of losing markets in the New World, but the political damage is lasting. **1947** President Truman issues Executive Order number 9835, calling for loyalty investigations of all federal employees. **1960** Arthur L. Schawlow and Charles H. Townes patent the laser.

✦ 23 ✦

1775 Patrick Henry calls on the Virginia Provincial Congress to put the colony on military alert. When there is opposition from Loyalists, he replies: "Is life so dear or peace so sweet as to be purchased at the price of chains and slavery? Forbid it, Almighty God! I know not what course others may take, but as for me, give me liberty or give me death!" **1971** Congress

MARCH 22
The hated stamp and an anonymous response to it. (Library of Congress)

MARCH 23

a tribute to Patrick Henry by an unknown painter of the early nineteenth century. (Shelburne Museum, Shelburne, Vermont)

proposes the Twenty-sixth Amendment, lowering the voting age in all United States elections to eighteen, after the Supreme Court had invalidated the Voting Age Act of 1970.

✦ 24 ✦

1668 The royal governor, Sir Edmund Andros, trying to restore the Crown's control in the rambunctious New England colonies, places the militias of New England under his direct control. Earlier in the year he had forbidden the towns to hold more than one meeting a year. **1765** The Quartering Act is issued to the thirteen colonies. Colonists must now provide for board and upkeep of British soldiers, supplying them with "candles, firing, bedding, cooking utensils, salt and vinegar, and five pints of small beer or cider, or a gill of rum per man, per diem." **1862** In Cincinnati visiting abolitionist Wendell Phillips is pelted with eggs and rocks after he calls for emancipation of slaves to be made one of the goals of the Civil War. The official purpose of the war at this stage is to end the rebellion, not to abolish slavery.

✦ 25 ✦

1634 A group of colonists, under the aegis of Catholic Lord Baltimore, reaches the coast of Maryland after crossing from England aboard the *Dove* and the *Ark.* Mass is celebrated for the first time in the continental United States. **1894** Jacob Coxey leaves Massilon, Ohio, leading an "army" of about 100 unemployed. Their destination is Washington, D.C., where they hope their pleas for economic reform will be heard. **1911** A fire breaks out at the Triangle Shirtwaist Company in New York, which employs mostly immigrant women in sweatshop conditions. Because stairways are blocked, frantic girls leap from the blazing eighth and ninth floors. Before the fire is put out, over 145 lives are lost. **1931** In Scottsboro, Alabama, nine young black men are accused of raping two white women on a freight train. The men are quickly convicted, but the case is appealed and retried four more times, focusing the nation's attention on the condition of blacks in the South.

✦ 26 ✦

1602 Explorer Bartholomew Gosnold departs Falmouth, England, on a voyage that takes him to the New England coast, where, on May 15, he sights Cape Cod and gives it its name. **1790** Congress passes the Naturalization Act, requiring new immigrants to complete a two-year residence before they can become citizens. **1883** With a dress ball that sets new standards for conspicuous consumption, Mrs. William K. Vanderbilt inaugurates her mansion on Fifth Avenue and becomes a national symbol of the giddy pleasures of extravagant spending. Her daughter later wrote: "Now firmly established as a social leader, my mother, wishing still further to dominate her world, assumed the prerogatives of an *arbiter elegantiarum,* instructing her contemporaries both in the fine arts and the art of living."

✦ 27 ✦

1513 Ponce de Leon sites the land mass of Florida, names it, and claims it for the king of Spain. **1858** An evangelical movement known as the Great Revival sweeps through the major cities of the East. Financier George Templeton Strong, an Episcopalian, takes a dim view of the movement, speculating in his diary: "Business is dismally stagnant . . . and there is little sign of its revival. That fact has much to do with the existing 'Revival of Religion.' People miss their wonted excitement in Wall Street and seek a substitute in the sensations of a religious meeting." **1964** An earthquake strikes Alaska, registering 8.4 on the Richter scale. The severest earthquake recorded in North America (the San Francisco earthquake of 1906 is estimated at 8.25), it destroys Anchorage's downtown business section, and 114 lives are lost.

MARCH 25

The tragic aftermath of the Triangle fire, when fire engine ladders were unable to reach the upper stories and workers jumped to their deaths. The fire led to efforts to develop equipment to fight skyscraper fires. (Brown Brothers)

✦ **28** ✦

1841 Dorothea Dix takes charge of a women's Sunday school class at a Boston prison. After touring the facility, she is so shocked by the hellish conditions that she resolves to dedicate her life to social reform. Over the next three years, she visits over 300 prisons and over 500 poorhouses and writes articles exposing the hellish conditions she observes. **1881** Master showman P. T. Barnum goes into partnership with his major rival, James A. Bailey of the Great London Circus, to create a mammoth extravaganza, the Barnum and London Circus. "Old showmen declared that we could never take in enough money to cover our expenses, which would be fully forty-five hundred dollars per day." **1979** An accident at the Three Mile Island nuclear power plant near Harrisburg, Pennsylvania, sends clouds of radioactive steam into the atmosphere, although a meltdown is averted.

MARCH 26

Alva Vanderbilt costumed with stuffed doves for her ball. (New-York Historical Society)

THE RUSSIAN SETTLEMENT

RECEIVED
WITH OPEN ARMS

THE FISH
BITE QUITE FREELY

THE OFFICIAL SEAL

MARCH 30
Harper's Weekly on the Alaska Purchase.

✦ 29 ✦

1638 The first Swedish immigrants to the New World arrive at Fort Christina, present site of Wilmington, Delaware, bringing with them designs for the log cabin and steambath. **1790** John Tyler, tenth president of the United States, is born in Greenway, Virginia. He will be the first to gain office because of the incumbent's death, and his right to succession will be challenged in Congress, where a resolution is introduced to give him the title of acting president. His political enemies referred to President Tyler as "His Accidency." **1973** The last American combat troops leave South Vietnam.

✦ 30 ✦

1791 Construction begins on the Knoxville Road, a turnpike that will link Virginia's Wilderness Road to the frontier. **1867** Secretary of State Seward reaches agreement with the czarist government of Russia to purchase the territory of Alaska for $7.2 million, which works out to about 2 cents an acre. **1981** President Ronald Reagan and three aides are shot and wounded outside a Washington, D.C., hotel. The gunman, a young man with no apparent motive named John W. Hinckley, Jr., is found by the courts to be criminally insane.

A contemporary Japanese print of Commodore Perry meeting the Japanese high commissioners. (United States Naval Academy Museum)

✦ 31 ✦

1776 Abigail Adams writes to her husband John, then involved in setting a framework for the new nation: "In the new code of laws which I suppose it will be necessary for you to make, I desire you would remember the ladies and be more generous and favorable to them than your ancestors." **1840** A ten-hour day is established for federal public works employees. Factory workers at the time were working an average of 11.4 hours a day. **1854** In Kanagawa, Japan, Commodore Matthew Perry negotiates a treaty that opens key Japanese ports to American traders. **1940** *Oklahoma!* by Richard Rodgers and Oscar Hammerstein II opens on Broadway.

April

HOW TO SHOP WITH WAR RATION BOOK TWO
.. to Buy Canned, Bottled and Frozen Fruits and Vegetables; Dried Fruits, Juices and all Canned Soups

YOUR POINT ALLOWANCE MUST LAST FOR THE FULL RATION PERIOD
Plan How Many Points You Will Use Each Time *Before* You Shop

BUY EARLY IN THE WEEK   Foods are going to our fighting men. They come first! Your ration gives you your fair share of the foods that are left.   BUY EARLY IN THE DAY

APRIL *22 (Opening illustration)*
The Oklahoma Land Rush, a mural by
John Steuart Curry, gives a festive
cast to a bittersweet event in the
opening of the frontier. (Department
of the Interior)

APRIL 1
Wartime rationing operated on a
point system, as explained in this
Office of Price Administration poster.
(AP/Wide World Photos)

✦ 1 ✦

1826 Captain Samuel Mory of Orford, New Hampshire, receives a patent for a two-cylinder internal combustion engine. **1913** It was "along about April 1, 1913," wrote Henry Ford (in 1923) that he installed his first moving assembly line. **1943** Meats, cooking oil, and cheese are placed under wartime rationing. **1945** The invasion of Okinawa, code named Operation Iceberg, begins with the landing of more than 450,000 U.S. troops. Because Japanese defenders are hiding inland, there is little resistance the first day. **1946** The United Mine Workers go on strike, part of a widespread movement by organized labor, including steelworkers, auto workers, and trainmen, to catch up on the raises and benefits that were deferred during the war years. **1954** The Air Force Academy is established at a site near Colorado Springs, Colorado.

✦ 2 ✦

1819 *The American Farmer,* the first successful agricultural journal in the United States, begins publication in Baltimore. **1878** The Women's Hotel, first in the nation to cater to unescorted women, opens in New York City. **1902** The nation's first motion picture theater opens in Los Angeles. **1917** President Wilson calls Congress into special session to ask for a declaration of war against Germany. "The world must be made safe for democracy," he declares.

APRIL 1
Model T bodies being mounted on
chassis, about 1914. (Detail, Henry
Ford Museum and Greenfield Village)

IL. 3

...s painted buffalo hide robe, de-
...ting an attack on the Mandans by
...ux and Arikaras, was among the
...ns sent to President Jefferson by
...vis and Clark in 1805. (Peabody
...useum, Harvard University)

✦ 3 ✦

1805 The Lewis and Clark expedition, in what is now North Dakota, collects animal, bird, and plant specimens for their sponsor, Thomas Jefferson, and sends ten men off to Washington to present the items to the president. **1860** The Pony Express begins its brief but historic courier service, delivering mail from Missouri to California in eight days. The completion of a transcontinental telegraph line in 1861 will put the mounted couriers out of business. **1865** Union troops enter the Confederate capital at Richmond, which has been set afire by retreating Confederate troops. **1893** Thomas F. Bayard becomes the first person appointed to the newly created rank of ambassador. He is ambassador to Great Britain.

✦ 4 ✦

1775 The *Pennsylvania Mercury* becomes the first newspaper to be printed from American-made type. **1818** Congress decides to restore the American flag to its original thirteen stripes and from now on add only new stars when a new state joins the Union. **1949** The North Atlantic Treaty Organization pact is signed in Washington, D.C., creating a defensive alliance of North American and West European nations. **1968** In Memphis, where he had gone to lend support to a garbage workers' strike, the Reverend Dr. Martin Luther King, Jr., is assassinated.

Peary photographed his crew at the North Pole; Matthew Henson, center holds an American flag. (Admiral Robert E. Peary/Edward P. Stafford)

✦ 5 ✦

1614 The Jamestown colony tobacco planter, John Rolfe, marries Pocahontas, daughter of the hitherto hostile chief Powhatan; she had converted to Christianity while being held hostage. **1764** The British Parliament passes the Revenue Act, known as the Sugar Act although it imposes taxes on a number of imports, including coffee and textiles. To the British the law seems a way to combat smuggling, but colonial merchants consider it discriminatory and provocative. **1851** Mayor Ambrose Kingsland of New York proposes to the Common Council that a large park be built in Manhattan to provide a healthful recreational center for the city's people—a kind of safety valve, according to enlightened social theory, for the tensions caused by urban life. After much political maneuvering, construction begins in 1856 on Central Park.

✦ 6 ✦

1830 The government of Mexico bans American settlers from its Texas province and abolishes slavery. **1862** At Pittsburg Land, Tennessee, near Shiloh Church, 40,000 Confederate troops attack the Union encampment while General Grant is absent, taking the soldiers by surprise. A massacre seems possible until the attackers lose momentum while fighting in a grove of trees known as the Hornet's Nest. **1909** Robert E. Peary, his assistant, Matthew Henson, and four Eskimoes arrive at latitude 90 degrees north, the North Pole. They are the first people known to reach the Pole. **1917** Jeannette Rankin, the first woman to sit in Congress, makes her debut speech by voting against America's participation in World War I. "I want to stand by my country," she says, "but I cannot vote for war." She was later to vote against entry into World War II as well, the only member of Congress to do so.

✦ **7** ✦

1862 On the second day of fighting at Shiloh, General Grant returns and Union reinforcements arrive, including a division under General Lew Wallace (later the author of *Ben-Hur*). Outnumbered and disorganized, the Confederates retreat, although they nearly destroyed Grant's army the day before. **1922** Interior Secretary Albert B. Fall leases Naval Reserve No. 3, "Teapot Dome," to oilman Harry F. Sinclair, even though it had been set aside for military use. Fall was later discovered to have received a $25,000 "loan" from Sinclair. **1927** Secretary of Commerce Herbert Hoover appears on screen in the first successful demonstration of television.

✦ **8** ✦

1789 The new House of Representatives gathers to consider the first item on its agenda: how the new government can raise money. **1793** The minister of the revolutionary French Republic, Edmond Charles Édouard Genêt, known as Citizen Genêt, arrives in Charleston and almost immediately causes distress by commissioning privateers to attack British ships off the U.S. coast and encouraging expeditions into Florida and Louisiana. **1826** The quarrel between Secretary of State Henry Clay and fiery Virginia Senator John Randolph culminates in a duel. Both men misfire, but the feud continues. As it simmers, the Democratic-Republican Party comes apart, with the Adams-Clay wing becoming the Whig Party and the Jackson wing becoming the Democratic Party.

APRIL 6

...sk on April 6 at Pittsburg Land-...g, as Union troops, pushed to the ...ge of the Tennessee River, try to ...group and hold off the day's last ...onfederate assault. (Print Division, ...ew York Public Library)

✦ 9 ✦

1682 Robert Cavelier, Sieur de La Salle, reaches the mouth of the Mississippi and claims the territory, which he names Louisiana, for Louis XIV. **1865** General Robert E. Lee surrenders to General Grant at Appomattox Court House, Virginia. Grant tells his men: "The war is over—the rebels are our countrymen again." **1939** Shut out of the DAR's Constitution Hall, where she had planned to give a concert, black contralto Marian Anderson performs for an audience of 75,000 on the steps of the Lincoln Memorial.

✦ 10 ✦

1790 The Patent Act creates a three-member board of approval, one of whom is Thomas Jefferson, to consider licenses for new inventions. **1841** Horace Greeley begins publishing the *New York Tribune,* a paper he builds into a powerful voice for his opinions, especially on slavery. **1849** The safety pin is patented by inventor Walter Hunt, who quickly sells the patent rights for $100. **1866** The American Society for the Prevention of Cruelty to Animals is chartered in New York. **1877** President Hayes begins withdrawing federal troops from the South, marking the end of Reconstruction. **1916** The first professional golf tournament is held at the Siwanoy course in Bronxville, New York. **1942** Seventy-five thousand U.S. and Philippine troops captured on Bataan the day before begin the six-day "death march" to prison camp. Almost half of the 12,000 Americans die on the march.

APRIL 9

Marian Anderson at her Lincoln Memorial concert, 1939. (Thomas McAvoy/*Life Magazine* © 1939 Time Inc.)

APRIL 9

A pencil drawing by Alfred B. Wau of General Lee leaving the McLean house after surrendering. "It was impossible to say," wrote Grant, "whether he felt inwardly glad that the end had finally come, or felt sa over the result, and was too manly to show it. Whatever his feelings, they were entirely concealed from my observation." (Library of Congress)

✦ 11 ✦

1789 The tradesmen of Baltimore petition Congress to request tariff protection: "Since the close of the last war, and the completion of the Revolution, the petitioners have observed the manufacturing and trading interests of the country rapidly declining, while the wealth of the people hath been prodigally expended in the purchase of those articles, from foreigners, which our citizens, if properly encouraged, were fully competent to finish." **1816** The Reverend Richard Allen, an ex-slave, is ordained as bishop of the newly created African Methodist Episcopal Church in Philadelphia, which Allen helped found as a protest against racial divisions in the Methodist church. **1951** General Douglas MacArthur is fired as commander in chief of the U.S. Army in Korea after his public disagreements with President Truman's policies had called into question the tradition of civilian control over the military.

✦ 12 ✦

1811 Fort Astoria, the first permanent American colony in the Pacific Northwest, is established at Cape Disappointment, Washington, by settlers from New York who name the place after their sponsor, the fur trader John Jacob Astor. **1843** A charter to sell life insurance is granted the Mutual Life Insurance Company of New York, launching the American industry. **1861** After months of uncertainty the shooting begins: Confederate batteries in Charleston Harbor open fire on Fort Sumter, which surrenders the next day, with no lives lost.

APRIL 10
Beginning of the Bataan death march.
(AP/Wide World Photos)

✦ 13 ✦

1743 Thomas Jefferson is born in Shadwell, Virginia. "The only birthday I ever commemorate is that of our Independence, the Fourth of July," he remarks when he is president. **1830** A Washington political dinner commemorating Jefferson's birthday becomes a symbolic battleground. President Andrew Jackson rises to give a toast and, looking at his vice president, John C. Calhoun, a states-rights man, proclaims: "Our Federal Union—it must be preserved!" Calhoun rises and toasts: "The Union—next to our liberty, the most dear!" **1869** George Westinghouse receives a patent for the steam power brake, which makes it possible to run longer trains.

✦ 14 ✦

1865 President Lincoln is shot at Ford's Theater in Washington by the actor John Wilkes Booth, who cries out "*Sic semper tyrannis! The South is avenged.*" Lincoln dies the next day, aged fifty-six, the first president to be assassinated. **1894** Thomas Edison's device for showing moving pictures, a peepshow machine called the Kinetoscope, is given its first public exhibition in New York City. **1912** On its maiden voyage the luxury liner *Titanic* strikes an iceberg and sinks. Supposedly unsinkable, the ship lacks sufficient lifeboats, and 1,502 people go down with it. Back in America, young David Sarnoff relays messages of the sinking from his wireless station, which makes the public aware of the lifesaving potential of this new medium. **1935** Troubadour folksinger Woody Guthrie, traveling across Texas, witnesses a dust storm and is inspired to write one of his Dust Bowl Ballads, *So Long, It's Been Good to Know Yuh.*

APRIL 14

A British advertisement of 1912 that, however briefly, used the *Titanic* as exemplar of luxury and elegance. (Bryan Holme)

APRIL 16

Andrew Carnegie. (Culver Pictures)

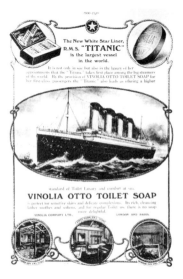

APRIL 14
Dust storm, Cimarron County, Oklahoma, 1936, photographed by Arthur Rothstein. (Library of Congress)

✦ 15 ✦

1788 The *Salem* (Massachusetts) *Mercury* reports the departure of the brig *Cadet,* bound for Madeira. After two years the *Cadet* will return to Boston with a cargo of pepper, having discovered the Dutch East India Company's source and broken a 122-year monopoly. **1822** After advertising in a local paper for "enterprising young men," William Ashley and Andrew Henry lead a trapping expedition out of St. Louis that includes the legendary mountain men Jedediah Smith and William Bridger. Their destination is the source of the Missouri, over 2,500 miles away in Montana. **1952** The Franklin National Bank of New York issues the nation's first bank credit card. **1959** Fidel Castro, Cuba's new ruler, begins an unofficial eleven-day goodwill tour of the United States and Canada.

✦ 16 ✦

1787 General Washington's name heads the subscription list for Royall Tyler's *The Contrast,* which has its first performance at New York City's John Street Theater. This comedy, which ridicules aristocracy, is considered the first professionally produced American play with American subject matter. **1901** The Minnesota Abrasive Company, forerunner of Minnesota Mining and Manufacturing Company, is incorporated to mine corundum. **1905** Andrew Carnegie, who wrote in 1889 that "the man who dies rich, dies disgraced," continues his program of philanthropic divestiture by establishing the Carnegie Foundation for the Advancement of Teaching. **1926** Book-of-the-Month Club distributes its first Selection, Sylvia Townsend Warner's *Lolly Willowes,* to 4,750 charter members.

APRIL 19

Paul Revere's Ride, by an unknown folk artist. (CBS, Inc.)

APRIL 18

Chinatown in San Francisco after the 1906 earthquake. (Library of Congress)

✦ 17 ✦

1830 In Baltimore abolitionist William Lloyd Garrison begins a jail sentence after proving unable to pay a $50 fine. Garrison was convicted for his remarks about a shipowner who transported slaves. Such men, he said, were "enemies of their own species." **1933** Camp Roosevelt, the first Civilian Conservation Corps camp, opens in Luray, Virginia. Modeled after a reforestation project Franklin Roosevelt had introduced while governor of New York, the CCC will put 2.5 million men under twenty-five—mostly city boys—to work, paying them $35 per month, of which $25 had to be sent home.

✦ 18 ✦

1775 British commander in chief General Thomas Gage orders a unit of Regulars to march from Boston to Concord to seize supplies of arms and ammunition stored there by the colony. Word leaks out, and two Americans, William Dawes and Paul Revere, head out separately on horseback to warn that the British are on the way. **1842** In the event known as Dorr's Rebellion, Rhode Island voters who were disenfranchised by a property-owning requirement hold their own elections and choose Thomas W. Dorr as governor. "So the smallest state of the Union is the only one which can boast of *two* governors," wrote diarist Philip Hone a few days later. **1906** A massive earthquake strikes San Francisco, followed by fires that burn for three days. Over 500 people are killed, at least 100,000 are left homeless, and almost 3,000 city acres are flattened.

✦ 19 ✦

1775 Early in the morning both Paul Revere and William Dawes are intercepted by a British patrol, but Samuel Prescott, a young doctor out courting, continues on ahead to warn the patriots. At sunrise the British reach Lexington common, where they are met by seventy armed Minutemen, whose commander, John Parker, orders his men to disperse. Someone opens fire, which is answered, and eight Minutemen are

APRIL 17

Leisure time at a CCC camp in George Washington National Forest, May 1933. (AP/Wide World Photos)

quickly killed and ten wounded. The British proceed on to Concord, where there is stiffer fighting, and then retreat. **1861** Federal troops en route to Washington are attacked by Confederate sympathizers in Baltimore. Four men of the 6th Massachusetts Volunteers become the first casualties of the Civil War. The wounded are treated by Clara Barton, who takes the lead in organizing medical care for the Union soldiers.

✦ **20** ✦

1606 King James grants a group of merchants called the Virginia Company a charter to create two colonies in the new world—which turn out to be Jamestown and Plymouth—and to propagate the Gospel "to such People, as yet live in Darkness." **1837** Massachusetts creates a state board of education to implement social reformer Horace Mann's goal of universal public education: "Having found the present generation composed of materials almost unmalleable," Mann wrote, "I am about transferring my efforts to the next. Men are cast-iron; but children are wax."

✦ 21 ✦

1649 Maryland passes a Toleration Act that extends religious freedom to all Christians. In actual practice, Jews are tolerated as well. **1790** Twenty thousand people, said to be the largest public gathering in America, attend the burial service in Philadelphia of Benjamin Franklin, who died April 17. **1828** Former country schoolmaster Noah Webster publishes his *American Dictionary of the English Language.* Its 70,000 entries, including words derived from Indian and European languages, make it the largest English-language dictionary of the time. **1836** In the Battle of San Jacinto, Santa Ana's Mexican army is surprised and overwhelmed by Sam Houston's Texas rebels, seeking revenge for the massacre at the Alamo. As a result Mexico is forced to recognize the independence of the Texas republic.

✦ 22 ✦

1794 Pennsylvania abolishes capital punishment for all crimes except murder. **1889** Nearly 2 million acres of Indian land in the Oklahoma Territory are opened to white settlers, and by day's end an uninhabited prairie becomes Oklahoma City, population 10,000. With the firing of a starting gun, settlers rush forward to stake their claims. Those who didn't wait for the gun are called Sooners—and Oklahoma becomes known as the Sooner State. **1972** The planet Earth receives its own holiday as environmental activists gather to observe the first Earth Day.

✦ 23 ✦

1784 Congress adopts Thomas Jefferson's plan for extending government to the territories west of the Appalachians but drops his proposal that the land be organized into ten states with classical names like Metropotamia and Polypotamia. His Indian-derived proposals Michigania and Illinoia survive, however. **1896** Koster & Bial's Music Hall in New York City is the setting for a première of motion pictures projected onto a screen. The show includes films of surf breaking on a beach, a comic boxing match, and dancing girls. "All wonderfully real and singularly exhilarating," reports the *New York Times.*

✦ 24 ✦

1800 The Library of Congress is established, and its collection begins when Thomas Jefferson donates his private library. **1833** The Patent Office grants a patent for the soda fountain. **1913** The 792-foot Woolworth Building in New York, the world's tallest building, whose tower is modeled after the campanile of St. Marks in Venice, is dedicated from the White House as President Wilson presses a button to illuminate it.

APRIL 24
The Arctic Soda Water fountain by James W. Tufts, 1876. (New-York Historical Society)

APRIL 24

Woolworth's "Cathedral of Commerce"—a newspaper called it "the greatest mountain of steel and stone ever erected by man," and a local clergyman said it inspired "feelings too deep even for tears." (Collection Business Americana, Smithsonian Institution)

✦ 25 ✦

1507 The New World is given the name America by the Dutch geographer Martin Waldseemueller, who is under the impression that Amerigo Vespucci had discovered the continent. **1844** New York City man about town George Templeton Strong writes in his diary about a stroll through Brooklyn's Green-Wood Cemetery which, in the absence of city parks, is becoming a fashionable retreat: "Beautiful place it is, and they're hard at work improving it, putting it all in good order. When it's brought to the same high state of civilization with Mount Auburn, it will far surpass it." Cambridge's Mount Auburn Cemetery, with its winding paths and picturesque landscapes, has set the standard for parklike cemeteries near cities that otherwise make no allowance for greenery. **1862** Flag Officer David Glasgow Farragut's forces take New Orleans without resistance after 4,000 Confederate troops withdraw and leave the city defenseless. Farragut is rewarded with a promotion to rear admiral, the first admiral in United States history.

✦ 26 ✦

1607 The settlers of the Virginia Company sight land. Within a week they will enter Chesapeake Bay and erect a cross at a place they name Cape Henry. **1777** As the war with Britain rages on, Congressional Congress delegate John Adams writes: "Posterity! You will never know, how much it cost the present Generation, to preserve your freedom! I hope you will make good use of it." **1854** Massachusetts abolitionists found the Emigrant Aid Society to encourage slavery opponents to migrate to Kansas, where the slavery issue is to be settled by a vote. The first group of twenty-nine migrants leaves Boston July 30, to reach Kansas July 30, and on August 1 found the community of Lawrence. **1865** John Wilkes Booth, a fugitive since the assassination of President Lincoln, is shot dead near Bowling Green, Virginia.

✦ 27 ✦

1822 Ulysses S. Grant, the eighteenth president, is born in Point Pleasant, Ohio, where he will grow up burdened with the nickname "Useless." **1831** John Quincy Adams writes in his diary about a visit to former president James Monroe, now homeless and living with his son-in-law: "Mr. Monroe is a very remarkable instance of a man whose life has been a continued series of the most extraordinary good fortune, who has never met with any known disaster, has gone through a splendid career of public service, has received more pecuniary reward from the public than any man since the existence of the nation, and is now dying, at the age of seventy-two, in wretchedness and beggary."

AMERICI VESPVCII

AQVILO

Martin Waldseemueller's 1507 map of the world, in which the "terra incognita" is named for Amerigo Vespucci. (Map Division, New York Public Library)

Along with the dimout went a government campaign to make Americans more security conscious. This poster by Oliver Nelson shows a sailor drowning after a torpedo attack, presumably the result of careless conversation. (Life Picture Service, *Life Magazine* © Time Inc.)

✦ 28 ✦

1758 The nation's fifth president and the last from the group that led the Revolution, James Monroe, is born in Westmoreland County. **1788** Maryland ratifies the Constitution and becomes the seventh state of the Union. **1818** A treaty known as the Rush-Bagot Agreement, after its negotiators, makes neutral the waters of the Great Lakes and establishes an unfortified frontier between the United States and Canada. **1834** Jason Lee, a recent Methodist convert, joins a wagon train leaving Missouri for the Oregon territory. There he founds the territory's first agricultural settlement and heads a mission to the Indians that spends $250,000 over the next eleven years without converting a single soul. **1942** A nightly "dim-out" begins along the East Coast now that the United States is officially at war.

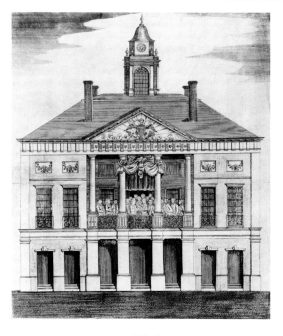

✦ 29 ✦

1842 Eighteen-year-old Francis Parkman writes to Jared Sparks, a Harvard College history professor, seeking advice on a research project, but unaware, of course, that the undertaking would occupy most of his life and be carried on during periods of near-blindness, until its seven volumes raised the writing of American history to its greatest heights: "I am desirous of studying the history of the Seven Years' War, and find it difficult to discover authorities sufficiently minute to satisfy me. I wish particularly to know the details of the military operations around Lake George—the characters of the officers—the relations of the Indian tribes—the history, the more minute the better, of partisan exploits—in short, all relating to the incidents of war in that neighborhood. Could you furnish me through the Post Office with the names of such authorities as you can immediately call to mind, you would do me a great kindness. Yours with great respect, F. Parkman, *Soph. Class.*"

✦ 30 ✦

1789 George Washington is inaugurated as president of the United States in New York City. Washington, who had hoped to retire to Mount Vernon, holds the office for seven years and ten months. **1812** The state of Louisiana is admitted to the Union as the eighteenth state. **1900** In Vaughan, Mississippi, locomotive engineer Casey Jones becomes a hero and a legend: Jones stays with his train, the Cannonball Express, when the

track is blocked, and slows it down enough to save the passengers, but not himself. **1939** The National Broadcasting Company begins regular television programming. The new medium seems unlikely to overtake radio, however, according to Harvard engineer Chester L. Dawes: "Television viewing is limited to a few persons, it must take place in a semi-darkened room, and it demands continuous attention."

May

MAY 1 *(Opening illustration)*
The White City of the Chicago
World's Fair, looking east from the
Grand Plaza. (Charles Dudley Ar-
nold/Avery Architectural and Fine
Arts Library, Columbia University)

MAY 1
In her eighties, Mother Jones
summed up her life: "I was born c
the struggle and the torment and t
pain. A child of the wheel, a brat c
the cogs, a woman of the dust. . .
When a laborer sweats his sweat of
blood and weeps his tears of blood
remedy is thrust upon the world. I
am the remedy." (Archives of Labo
and Urban Affairs, Wayne State Ur
versity)

✦ 1 ✦

1794 Philadelphia's shoemakers organize as the Federal Society
of Journeymen Cordwainers, considered the nation's first trade
union. **1867** Post Civil War voter registration begins in the
South. By the end of October, 1,363,000 voters will be registered, including 700,000 blacks. Alabama, Florida, Louisiana,
Mississippi, and South Carolina show black majorities. **1893**
The World's Columbian Exposition opens in Chicago, which
has been spectacularly rebuilt since its great fire. **1930** On her
100th birthday, Mother (Mary Harris) Jones, the fiery labor
organizer who was the soul of many a mine strike, gives her last
public speech. **1931** The world's tallest skyscraper, the Empire State Building, opens.

✦ 2 ✦

1676 Mary Rowlandson, a Massachusetts minister's wife seized
by Indians during King Phillip's War, is ransomed after eleven
weeks of captivity. Her memoir of the experience, one of the
first of a popular American genre, is reprinted about thirty
times. **1863** At Chancellorsville, Virginia, where Union General Joseph Hooker had taken a defensive position in a forest,
General Lee, outnumbered almost 2 to 1, divides his army and
sends General Stonewall Jackson to march around Hooker's
right flank, taking Hooker's men by surprise. During a lull in
the fighting Jackson is fatally wounded by by one of his own
men.

✦ 3 ✦

1666 In the face of an oversupply and a falling market, Maryland bans the commercial production of tobacco for one year. **1765** Dr. John Morgan is proposed as the first faculty member of the first medical school in the colonies, the College of Physicians of Philadelphia. **1845** Macon B. Allen, the first black lawyer admitted to the bar, passes his examination in Worcester, Massachusetts. **1942** In the Coral Sea near southern New Guinea, the aircraft carriers *Yorktown* and *Lexington* rendezvous and launch air strikes against the Japanese. Thus begins the first naval battle conducted entirely by planes from carriers. By May 8 both the *Yorktown* and *Lexington* are damaged, but seven Japanese warships are destroyed.

✦ 4 ✦

1626 Peter Minuit arrives in New Amsterdam to take up his duties as the first director general of New Netherlands. **1886** As police move in to break up a labor protest rally in Chicago's Haymarket Square, someone throws a bomb. Over sixty people are wounded, seven fatally. The police open fire on the crowd. In days to come the Haymarket Massacre is seized upon as evidence of an anarchist conspiracy threatening the civil order of the nation. The *New York Times* reports that no event since the Civil War has aroused so much public concern. **1970** At Kent State University in Ohio, national guardsmen called in to control a student antiwar demonstration open fire, killing four students and wounding nine.

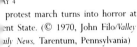

MAY 4
protest march turns into horror at Kent State. (© 1970, John Filo/*Valley Daily News*, Tarentum, Pennsylvania)

✦ 5 ✦

1865 A locomotive is overturned and robbed at North Bend, Ohio, in America's first recorded train robbery. **1925** The stage is set for a national debate as high school teacher John T. Scopes is arrested in Dayton, Tennessee, and charged with violating a state law against the teaching of evolution. **1945** An Oregon woman and five children are killed by a bomb that falls from a Japanese balloon, one of several balloon bombs directed against the U.S. Pacific coast. These are the only World War II fatalities to occur on the United States mainland. **1960** Two weeks before a crucial summit meeting, Soviet Premier Nikita Khrushchev announces that an American U-2 spy plane has been shot down over Soviet territory. **1961** The first American astronaut, Navy Commander Alan B. Shepard, Jr., travels 115 miles into space aboard the Mercury capsule *Freedom VII*.

✦ 6 ✦

1793 Debt-ridden artist Gilbert Stuart returns to the United States after a sojourn in England, having explained to a friend: "When I cann nett a sum sufficient to take me to America, I shall be off to my native soil. There I expect to make a fortune by Washington alone. I calculate upon making a plurality of his portraits." Back home, Stuart became a prisoner of his success, spending much of his career fulfilling commissions for copies of his Washington portraits. **1935** President Franklin Roosevelt creates the Works Progress Administration, his major effort at putting the nation back to work. About 30 percent of the unemployed will be hired to build schools, hospitals, and playgrounds, at an average salary of $55 per month.

MAY 8

The *Morning Bell* by Winslow Homer gives an idyllic picture of young mill girls on their way to work. (Francis G. Mayer, Art Color Slides, Inc.)

✦ 7 ✦

1789 The Protestant Episcopal Church is formed as an American counterpart to the Church of England, which is no longer welcome as such. The new church continues to use the Church of England's Book of Common Prayer. **1847** The American Medical Association is formed in Philadelphia to oversee training methods and upgrade the status of the profession. **1915** Six days after a warning from the German Embassy that Americans in the European war zone would be subject to attack, a German submarine fires without warning on the British liner *Lusitania,* which sinks off the Irish coast with 128 Americans among the 1,198 killed. **1945** In a school in Rheims, France, German military leaders surrender to General Dwight D. Eisenhower. "The mission of this Allied force was fulfilled at 0241, local time, May 7, 1945," Ike announces.

✦ 8 ✦

1792 Congress passes a conscription act requiring militia service of "every free able-bodied white male citizen." **1874** Massachusetts adopts a ten-hour workday for women. **1884** Harry S. Truman, thirty-third President of the United States, is born on a farm in Lamar, Missouri. "Some of the presidents were great and some of them weren't," he said in a 1959 interview. "I can say that because I wasn't one of the great presidents, but I had a good time trying to be one." **1886** Dr. John Styth Pemberton perfects the syrup for a soft drink that will be sold under the trademark Coca Cola. **1945** Celebrations across America and Europe mark VE Day, the end of the war in Europe.

✦ 9 ✦

1837 A financial panic has struck the investment community, diarist George Templeton Strong reports: "There's a run on all the banks, the depositors drawing out the specie as fast as tellers can count it. They are in a dangerous situation most certainly, and if they break we shall have a revolution here." The next day banks suspend specie payment. By year's end over 600 banks fail, and the ensuing depression lasts seven years. **1914** President Wilson proclaims the first Mother's Day, following a campaign by newspapers, politicians, clergymen, and a West Virginia woman named Ann Jarvis.

✦ 10 ✦

1775 Colonel Ethan Allen of Vermont and his Green Mountain Boys capture Fort Ticonderoga, the best-known British fort in North America, without a shot. As the news of Allen's feat spreads, people begin to think that defeating the British might not be so difficult after all. **1869** The Union Pacific and Central Pacific railroads join at Promontory, Utah, creating a transcontinental railway. The ceremony corrects a miscalculation: Earlier the two lines passed each other on parallel tracks because no one had specified a meeting point, but officials in Washington then selected Promontory as the meeting place.

✦ 11 ✦

1816 The American Bible Society is formed in New York, its purpose to combat secular trends by distributing Bibles as widely as possible. **1858** Minnesota becomes the thiry-second state of the Union. **1917** President Wilson receives a petition from the Central Committee of Negro College Men asking for an officers' training camp for blacks. Though desegregation of the army was their goal, "our young men are so anxious to serve their country in this crisis that they are willing to accept a separate camp." **1928** WGY in Schenectady, New York, announces the nation's first television schedule. The GE-owned station promises three broadcasts a week for a total of 1½ hours.

✦ 12 ✦

1789 The Society of Saint Tammany, which will become a symbol of the all-powerful political machine in the nineteenth century, begins innocuously as a fraternal organization for opponents of the Federalist Party. The club is named for a Delaware Indian chief who welcomed William Penn to America. **1864** In a torrential downpour Grant's army attacks Lee's fortifications at Spottsylvania, north of Richmond. Grant had told Lincoln, "I propose to fight it out on this line if it takes all summer."

MAY 10
The linkup of the Central Pacific's
Jupiter (left) and *No. 119* of the
Union Pacific at Promontory Point,
with the two chief engineers shaking
hands. The champagne bottles were
eliminated from reprints of the
photo. (Union Pacific Railroad Museum Collection)

Members of the first Japanese mission to the United States, 1860. (Brady Collection, National Archives)

✦ 13 ✦

1607 Captain John Smith and company drop anchor on a marshy peninsula in the James River and begin building a settlement the following day. Of the 144 passengers who left England, 105 have survived to found Jamestown, the first permanent English settlement in the New World. **1846** Congress grants President James Polk's request for a declaration of war with Mexico, which both supporters and opponents see as a way of expanding American territory. It is the first unpopular war in American history. **1889** President Benjamin Harrison appoints rising politician Theodore Roosevelt as his Civil Service commissioner, an unglamorous position that many think will end Roosevelt's career.

✦ 14 ✦

1804 "Under a jentle brease up the Missouri," according to their journals, the Lewis and Clark expedition departs from St. Louis to explore America's new acquisition, the Louisiana Territory, with instructions to seek "the most direct and practicable water communication across this continent for purposes of commerce." The party of forty, with a $2,500 grant from their sponsor, President Jefferson, is also to report on the "soil and face of the country" as well as the customs of the Indians. **1860** The first Japanese diplomats ever to pay a call on a

MAY 15
The U.S. mail takes to the air. (National Archives)

foreign country arrive in the United States. **1904** The first Olympic Games staged in the United States open in St. Louis as part of the Louisiana Purchase Exposition.

✦ 15 ✦

1852 Spiritualism has become a craze, notes diarist George Templeton Strong after visiting "Mrs. Fish and her knocking spirits" and examining the popular new books and newspapers in which "people publish statements of extraordinary visitations made them by six individuals 'in ancient costume,' who promenade about for a long while and finally disappear, leaving Hebrew and Sanscrit MSS behind them, not specially relevant to anything." **1918** Air mail service begins between New York City and Washington, D.C. **1942** Wartime gasoline rationing begins, with most civilians limited to three gallons a week. The measure is designed principally to save rubber, however, and black market gas is seldom hard to find.

✦ 16 ✦

1775 On the first occasion in American history in which a body of laws is put to a popular vote, Massachusetts voters reject a proposed Constitution. The document, revised by the provincial congress and put to a vote again, is ratified in June. **1866** Congress authorizes a new 5 cent coin, which is soon nicknamed the nickel. **1916** Congress proposes the Seventeenth Amendment, which calls for direct, popular election of U.S. senators, who have been chosen up to this point by state legislatures and were thus beholden to state officials. **1939** Rochester, New York, introduces a food stamp program that enables needy people to redeem coupons for surplus food. The idea will spread to 150 cities in the next two years.

✦ 17 ✦

1673 Father Marquette departs St. Ignace, Michigan, on an expedition of exploration and conversion led by the layman Louis Jolliet. Marquette gets to perform only one baptism, but later says that it alone made the trip worthwhile. **1792** The first meeting of what would become the New York Stock Exchange is held at the Merchants Coffee House in New York City. **1826** Wildlife artist John James Audubon, Haitian by birth, French by education, American by adoption, departs for England "with deep sorrow" because he cannot find a publisher here for his collection of bird drawings. **1875** *Aristides* wins the first running of the Kentucky Derby. **1954** The Supreme Court issues its ruling in *Brown* v. *the Board of Education:* "We conclude that in the field of public education the doctrine of 'separate but equal' has no place. Separate education facilities are inherently unequal."

✦ 18 ✦

1852 Massachusetts passes the nation's first school attendance law, requiring all children between the ages of eight and fourteen to attend. **1870** Kindergarten advocate Elizabeth Peabody writes to William Torrey Harris, superintendent of schools in St. Louis, requesting a meeting. St. Louis will become the first public school system to have a kindergarten. **1896** In *Plessy* v. *Ferguson,* the Supreme Court upholds Louisiana's segregation law by declaring that racial segregation is constitutional so long as "separate but equal" facilities are offered. **1926** The glamorous California evangelist Aimee Semple McPherson disappears from a beach at Venice, California. After weeks of rumors and hysteria among her thousands of followers, McPherson reappears on June 23 telling a story about a kidnapping ordeal. **1933** Congress passes the Tennessee Valley Act, which creates the nation's first public rural electrification project. **1980** Mount St. Helens, a volcano in Washington, erupts violently.

MAY 18
Aimee Semple McPherson, called "the world's most pulchritudinous evangelist," in Los Angeles. (AP/Wide World Photos)

MAY 20
A homesteader receiving the deed to her land. (California Historical Society/Title Insurance Collection of Historical Photographs, Los Angeles)

Wild Turkey, Plate I of Audubon's *The Birds of America,* which began publication in London in 1827. (New-York Historical Society)

✦ 19 ✦

1806 Charity schools in New York introduce the Lancastrian system, which cuts down on salaried teachers by using advanced pupils as monitors. The system raises visions of inexpensive mass education and is praised as the educational equivalent of the factory system in manufacturing. **1847** The *St. Joseph* (Missouri) *Gazette* lists the essential equipment for migrants to Oregon, including a yoke of oxen, two milk cows, and cattle for beef, but no furniture.

✦ 20 ✦

1785 The federal government makes its first land grant for education in a law that organizes the Western Reserve territory into townships, stipulating that one portion of every township be set aside for public schools. **1862** President Lincoln signs the Homestead Act, designed to stimulate settlement of the West by offering 160 acres of public land for a token payment to anyone who could farm a plot for five years and make basic improvements. **1873** A patent for riveted pocket pants is granted to Jacob Davis, a Reno tailor, and Levi Strauss, the proprietor of a dry goods store in San Francisco. Strauss' first sale of his patented blue denim pants with riveted pockets occurs the following year. **1932** Amelia Earhart becomes the first woman to cross the Atlantic solo. **1939** Pan American Airways begins the first scheduled commercial service across the Atlantic: A four-engine flying boat leaves Port Washington, Long Island, and reaches Lisbon twenty hours, sixteen minutes, later.

BRITANNIC. CELTIC. GERMANIC. ADRIATIC. BALTIC.
REPUBLIC. OCEANIC. GAELIC. BELGIC.

THESE WELL-KNOWN, FAST MAIL STEAMERS SAIL FROM

LIVERPOOL TO NEW YORK,
EVERY THURSDAY

MAY 23

"Steerage Accommodation Unequalled for Ventilation, Light, and Care for Passengers' Comfort," this White Star Line advertisement promises for passage from Liverpool to the United States in the 1880s. (National Park Service)

✦ 21 ✦

1787 Maryland recognizes the remarkable inventive talents of Oliver Evans by granting him a statewide monopoly on certain projects, including "a steam carriage for the purpose of conveying without the aid of animal force" and a system of automatic conveyers installed in Thomas Ellicott's Baltimore grain mill. Evans' system of conveyors, elevators, and hoppers was a totally mechanized operation, with watermills supplying power and human labor needed only to begin the operation. His steam engine design was used in industry but never developed for transport, in part because he was refused permission to use it on the Pennsylvania Turnpike, where it would have frightened the horses. **1878** D. A. Buck receives a patent for a mass-produced, low-cost watch. Within ten years a half million Waterbury watches were sold annually at $3.50–$4.00. **1881** Clara Barton founds the American Red Cross as a branch of the International Red Cross. **1927** Charles Lindbergh completes his 33½-hour solo transatlantic flight aboard the *Spirit of St. Louis.*

✦ 22 ✦

1856 In an incident which shocks the nation Senator Charles Sumner of Massachusetts, an outspoken opponent of slavery, is attacked with a cane and beaten on the Senate floor by Preston S. Brooks, South Carolina member of the House. **1843** A party of 1,000 men, women, and children leaves Independence, Missouri, to settle in Oregon. Trappers, traders, and missionaries had gone that way before, but this is the first large-scale migration west. **1959** Benjamin O. Davis, Jr., of the U.S. Air Force becomes America's first black major general. His father was the first black general in the regular Army.

✦ 23 ✦

1611 Sir Thomas Dale, new governor of the struggling colony at Jamestown, imposes martial law on the settlers in the hope that strict discipline will rescue the colony's fortunes. **1788** South Carolina ratifies the Constitution and becomes the eighth state. **1904** A price war breaks out among European steamship companies competing for immigrant passengers, and the price of a steerage ticket to America falls to $10. **1955** The Presbyterian General Assembly accepts women ministers, and in October the Reverend Margaret Towner is ordained.

✦ 24 ✦

1844 "What hath God wrought?" exclaims Samuel F. B. Morse in the first message sent over his invention, the telegraph. Dolley Madison, widow of President Madison, is a guest at the Washington ceremony, and is invited to send the next message: "Message from Mrs. Madison. She sends her love to Mrs. Wethered." **1856** In Kansas, where fighting has broken out between pro- and antislavery factions, radical abolitionist John Brown leads an attack on a community called Pottawatomie that results in the death of five proslavery men. **1893** In Oberlin, Ohio, the Reverend H. H. Russell founds the Anti-Saloon League, which gives new impetus to the movement to outlaw drinking.

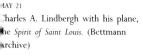

MAY 21

Charles A. Lindbergh with his plane, the *Spirit of Saint Louis*. (Bettmann Archive)

✦ 25 ✦

1539 Fernando de Soto, governor of Cuba, sails to Florida and lands at Tampa Bay, claiming the region for Spain. His party includes Francisca Hintestrosa, wife of one of his soldiers, who is thought to be the first woman colonist in North America. **1721** John Copson of Philadelphia begins the first marine and fire insurance company in America. **1787** Delegates of the thirteen states meet in Philadelphia to revise the Articles of Confederation, mindful of Washington's warning that "something must be done or the fabric will fall." Out of their deliberations will come not merely a revision of the system, but a new Constitution. **1793** Stephen Theodore Badin, a refugee from revolutionary France, becomes the first priest ordained in the United States at a ceremony in Baltimore.

✦ 26 ✦

1854 The first damaging break in the Missouri Compromise of 1820 occurs when Congress passes Stephen Douglas' Kansas-Nebraska Act, which opens the question of slavery to a vote in two newly created territories, Kansas and Nebraska. By the terms of the Missouri Compromise slavery would have been automatically prohibited that far north. **1876** General George Armstrong Custer leads his 655-man cavalry regiment out of Fort Lincoln, South Dakota, toward Little Big Horn. **1938** The House Committee to Investigate Un-American Activities is formed under the leadership of Texas Representative Martin Dies. Committee member Parnell Thomas announces an intention to focus on "the New Deal masterminds."

✦ 27 ✦

1647 Peter Stuyvesant is inaugurated governor of New Amsterdam, which has grown from a trading post to a thriving settlement but which faces increasing threats from neighboring British colonies. **1864** As General Lee tries to halt Grant's advance on Richmond and heavy destruction occurs in Sherman's Atlanta campaign, Mary Chesnut writes in her diary from Camden, South Carolina: "Our fighting men have all gone to the front. Only old men and little boys at home now. . . . It is impossible to sleep here because it is so solemn and still. The

MAY 28

Turtles by Jacques Burkhardt, from Volume II of Louis Agassiz' *Natural History of the United States of America.* (Museum of Comparative Zoology, Harvard University © President and Fellows of Harvard College)

MAY 27

Peter Stuyvesant, governor of New Amsterdam. (New-York Historical Society)

MAY 27

Oliver Wendell Holmes, Jr., then a Massachusetts judge, at ease on a summer tour. (Holmes Papers, Harvard Law School Library)

MAY 28

Rabbi Chaim Isaac Carigal, an itinerant preacher. (Beinecke Rare Book and Manuscript Library, Yale University)

moonlight shines in my window, sad and white." **1929** Judge Oliver Wendell Holmes, Jr., dissents from a Supreme Court ruling that denies citizenship to Rosa Schwimmer, a pacifist from Hungary: "If there is any principle of the Constitution that more imperatively calls for attachment than any other it is the principle of free thought—not free thought for those who agree with us but freedom for the thought that we hate. I think that we should adhere to that principle with regard to admission into, as well as life within, this country."

✦ 28 ✦

1767 The *New York Gazette and Weekly Post Boy* reports that French Huguenot refugees have settled in South Carolina and are cultivating the silkworm. **1773** The first sermon in a Jewish service in America is preached in Spanish by Rabbi Chaim Isaac Carigal at Newport's Touro Synagogue. Carigal is an itinerant preacher from Hebron in Palestine. **1830** President Andrew Jackson signs the Indian Removal Act, beginning the forced exile of Eastern Indians to the newly created Indian Territory in Oklahoma. **1855** Swiss immigrant Louis Agassiz, a pioneer in researching and teaching America's natural history, launches a campaign for support of his upreccedentedly thorough ten-volume natural history of the United States.

✦ 29 ✦

1699 The *Nassau,* commanded by Captain Giles Shelley, arrives at Cape May, New Jersey, with a full hold of cargo after a journey to Madagascar. But word leaks out that the captain has also brought back twenty-nine Red Sea pirates who plan to try their luck along the East Coast, precipitating a panic. **1790** Rhode Island, last of the original thirteen to ratify the Constitution, becomes the thirteenth state of the Union. **1843** John C. Frémont—soldier, adventurer, and future presidential hopeful—begins his second and most productive expedition to the West Coast. His party will survey an overland route to Oregon and study the geography of California and the Great Basin, all in the interest of strengthening U.S. claims to the Oregon Territory. **1848** Wisconsin becomes the thirtieth state of the Union. **1917** John Fitzgerald Kennedy, thirty-fifth president and first Roman Catholic to hold the office, is born in Brookline, Massachusetts.

✦ 30 ✦

1783 America's first daily newspaper, the *Pennsylvania Evening Post,* begins publication in Philadelphia. **1806** Andrew Jacksons kills a fellow lawyer, Charles Dickinson, in a duel pro-

MAY 29
John Charles Frémont exemplifying his nickname, "the Pathfinder," in the Rockies. (Library of Congress)

MAY 31
The Johnstown flood is spectacularly represented in this 1890 Kurz and Allison lithograph. (Philadelphia Print Shop, Ltd.)

voked by a personal insult. **1830** *Tom Thumb,* a one-horse-power locomotive built by businessman Peter Cooper, passes its first test by pulling over 4 tons at 15 miles per hour. **1868** The first Memorial Day is observed as General John A. Logan calls on soldiers and veterans to decorate military graves with flowers.

✦ 31 ✦

1689 Jacob Leisler, a trader working for the Dutch West India Company, leads an army of farmers in rebellion against English rule and seizes the British garrison in New York City, remaining in command until March 1691. **1790** Congress passes a national copyright law after lobbying by dictionary-maker Noah Webster, who was worried about the fate of his forthcoming *American Spelling Book.* (Webster's book would sell 15 million copies in his lifetime.) **1884** Dr. John Harvey Kellogg of Battle Creek, Michigan, applies for a patent on "flaked cereal and process of preparing same." **1889** The dam above Johnstown, Pennsylvania, breaks after heavy rains, and the town is buried under 30 feet of water, killing 2,295 people. **1913** The Seventeenth Amendment to the Constitution, providing for direct popular election of senators, becomes law, replacing nomination by state legislatures. **1918** Secretary of War Newton D. Baker offers military exemptions for conscientious objectors, who would be expected to do farm work without pay.

June

✦ 1 ✦

1660 Mary Dyer, Quaker friend of Anne Hutchinson, is hanged in Boston. Dyer's execution shocks many, and soon after, hanging for heretical preaching is prohibited by the king. **1792** Kentucky becomes the fifteenth state of the Union. **1796** Tennessee is admitted to the Union as the sixteenth state. **1821** Emma Willard, pioneer in higher education for women, founds the Waterford Academy for Young Ladies in Waterford, New York. Later she will establish the nation's first college-level school for women, the Troy, New York, Female Seminary. **1847** John Humphrey Noyes, a utopian evangelist, asks his followers, "Is not now the time for us to commence the testimony that the Kingdom of God is come?" and thereupon inaugurates a "complex marriage," or free love, colony at Putney, Vermont, which is later transferred to Oneida, New York.

✦ 2 ✦

1774 Parliament revises and revives the Quartering Act, which requires all the colonies to provide housing for the increasingly numerous British troops posted to America. **1851** The Maine legislature passes a law called "A Bill for the Suppression of Drinking Houses and Tippling Shops," by its author, Portland Mayor Neal Dow, "the Father of Prohibition." **1875** James A. Healy, the first black bishop of the Roman Catholic Church, is consecrated in Portland, Maine. **1924** All United States-born Indians are granted full American citizenship.

JUNE 3

The *Flying Cloud,* the fastest clipper of the day, in an 1855 Currier lithograph. (Peabody Museum of Salem)

JUNE 1

Emma Willard (Emma Willard School, Troy, New York)

JUNE 20 *(Opening illustration)*
The city of Washington seen from the heights above Georgetown. Painted by George Jacob Beck between 1795 and 1797, this is one of the earliest known views of the city. (Private collection)

JUNE 1
The men and women of Oneida work together sewing travel bags for sale outside the community. The women are wearing short skirts and pantaloons that John Humphrey Noyes designed. (Oneida Community Historical Committee)

✦ 3 ✦

1851 The *Flying Cloud,* by master shipbuilder Donald McKay, the largest merchant ship of its time and the most celebrated of all American clipper ships, departs Sandy Hook, New Jersey, on its maiden voyage to San Francisco. The trip sets a record time (89 days, 21 hours) for the New York to San Francisco route, where speed has been prized ever since the beginning of the Gold Rush. **1942** The Japanese attempt to seize the Pacific island of Midway results in the first major naval loss for Japan and is a critical turning point in the Pacific War. **1972** Sally Preisand, America's first woman rabbi, is ordained at the Isaac M. Wise Temple in Cincinnati.

✦ 4 ✦

1781 Jack Jouett completes a forty-five-mile ride to warn Virginia Governor Thomas Jefferson that the British are advancing on Charlottesville, giving Jefferson and the legislature time to escape. **1787** Delegates to the Constitutional Convention approve a single chief executive to govern the nation. It is understood that the first chief executive will be George Washington, but many delegates worry about who might follow. **1896** The first Ford automobile is assembled in Detroit, but a road test has to be postponed because the finished car is wider than the door of the shed in which it was built. **1944** General Dwight D. Eisenhower, commander of the long-planned Allied invasion of Europe, overrides the recommendations of Field Marshal Bernard Montgomery and orders that tomorrow's landing at Normandy be postponed until June 6, when the weather was predicted to clear.

Allied soldiers landing on the beach at Normandy: D Day. (UPI/Bettman Newsphotos)

✦ 5 ✦

1856 "We are 100 miles from a grist-mill, and 50 from a post office," writes Miriam Davis Colt about a vegetarian community in Kansas where the former teacher, her husband, and ninety-eight other idealists have settled. "The Indians have gone away now. . . ." she continues. "The people say we have had our hardest time here, but it does not seem so to me. I often ask myself, 'Why do I have so many presentiments of coming sorrow?'" After crop failure and sickness the family departs for St. Louis, but on the way her husband and son die from drinking bad water. Mrs. Colt's book, *Went to Kansas,* was published in 1862, by which time the colony was only a memory. **1947** In a speech at Harvard, Secretary of State George Marshall proposes a program of aid for rebuilding war-torn Europe, later known as the Marshall Plan. **1968** Senator Robert F. Kennedy, campaigning in Los Angeles for the Democratic Party's presidential nomination, is shot and killed.

✦ 6 ✦

1639 Edward Rauson is granted 500 acres at Pecoit, Massachusetts, to build a gunpowder mill, probably the first in America. **1822** An accidental shooting provides an opportunity for pioneering research in physiology by U.S. Army surgeon William Beaumont, who will study the digestive processes of a man whose abdominal wound left a fistulous opening in his stomach. **1944** "The eyes of the world are upon you," General Eisenhower tells the troops about to cross the English Channel to land on the beaches of Normandy. "The way home is via Berlin."

✦ 7 ✦

1769 Daniel Boone reaches Kentucky after a journey through the Cumberland Gap. In a few years he will found Boonesboro, one of the first settlements in the territory, and take a lead in the wars and treaties that wrest the land from the resident Indians. **1776** At the Continental Congress, Richard Henry Lee of Virginia speaks for the radical wing in offering a resolution: "That these United Colonies are, and of right ought to be, free and independent States, that they are absolved from all allegiance to the British Crown. . . ." The delegates postpone a decision but agree to form a committee to work out a declaration of independence. **1930** The *New York Times* announces that it will capitalize the *n* in "Negro" "in recognition of racial self-respect for those who have been for generations 'in the lower case.'"

✦ 8 ✦

1786 Commercially made ice cream is advertised in the *New York Gazette* by Mr. Hall of Chatham Street in New York City. **1869** A patent is awarded to Ives W. McGaffey of Chicago for his invention of a "sweeping machine" that operates by creating suction—a vacuum cleaner. **1905** The Pennsylvania Railroad announces eighteen-hour train service between New York and Chicago, and the New York Central follows a week later with its own eighteen-hour run, the *Twentieth Century Limited*. Some foresee the two cities becoming as close as suburbs, but both crack trains suffer fatal accidents in the first weeks of operation.

JUNE 8
This Victorian vacuum cleaner hardly looks like a laborsaving device.
(Brown Brothers)

✦ 9 ✦

1817 A boiler explosion destroys the innovative steamboat *Washington,* which, despite its fate, becomes a model for Mississippi River boats and the steamboats of the West. The *Washington*'s flat bottom and keelboatlike shallow hull gave it greater stability, and its machinery, which was placed on deck, achieved higher steam pressure and had greater capacity than the boats modeled after Fulton's prototype. **1860** Publisher Erastus Beadle issues the first dime novel, "a dollar book for a dime," *Malaeska: The Indian Wife of the White Hunter,* by historical novelist Ann Sophia Stephens. The book sells 300,000 copies in a year and is followed by hundreds of dime novels about frontiersmen, Indians, train robbers, and chaste heroines. **1943** The Internal Revenue Service introduces tax withholding, calling it the Pay As You Go Act.

✦ 10 ✦

1652 In defiance of British law America's first mint is established in Boston and begins issuing the pine tree shilling. **1768** Customs officers in Boston seize a ship owned by merchant John Hancock. Protesters gather and attack them on shore, and the next day the officials retreat to a fortified island in Boston harbor. **1861** Dorothea Dix is appointed superintendent of women nurses serving the Union Army. **1935** Alcoholics Anonymous is founded in New York City.

✦ 11 ✦

1776 After voting to formally declare independence from Britain, the Continental Congress appoints a committee to draw up a statement. The members appointed to work on this declaration of independence are Thomas Jefferson of Virginia, Benjamin Franklin of Pennsylvania, Roger Sherman of Connecticut, and Robert R. Livingston of New York. Jefferson is asked to prepare the first draft. **1816** The Gas Light Company of Baltimore is founded to illuminate the city's streets with coal gas lamps.

✦ 12 ✦

1776 Anticipating the national government by fifteen years, the Virginia assembly creates a Bill of Rights, including a provision for freedom of religion written by Patrick Henry: "Religion . . . can be directed only by reason and conviction, not by force or violence; and therefore all men are equally entitled to the free exercise of religion, according to the dictates of conscience." **1963** Medgar Evers, a civil rights leader and secretary of the NAACP, is murdered by a sniper in Jackson, Mississippi.

JUNE 10

Dorothea Dix; George Templeton Strong, who served with Dix on the Sanitary Commission, forerunner of the Red Cross, commented, "Working on her own, she does good, but no one can cooperate with her, for she belongs to the class of comets and can be subdued into relations with no system whatever." (Library of Congress)

his R. G. A. Levinge painting shows paddle steamer from about 1836, *uishita,* providing picturesque trans- ortation on the Red River, Louisiana erritory. (Amon Carter Museum, ort Worth, Texas)

✦ 13 ✦

1786 From Paris, Thomas Jefferson sends home his design, based on classical models, for a Virginia state capitol. Jefferson's classic revival style is quickly accepted as the way public buildings in the new republic should look. **1857** Edward M. Gallaudet arrives in Washington as superintendent at the Columbia Institution of the Deaf, Dumb and Blind, recently established by Congress. Gallaudet is the son of Thomas Hopkins Gallaudet, who pioneered education for the deaf in the United States, and the brother of the Reverend Thomas Gallaudet, who in 1852 opened a church for the deaf in New York City. **1861** Without enthusiasm President Lincoln agrees to the creation of a civilian sanitary commission to assist the military medical corps. There is little sense at the time that this will help the Union win the war and lead to the formation of the American Red Cross. **1966** The Supreme Court hands down its decision in *Miranda* v. *Arizona,* ruling that criminal suspects must be advised of their rights before they can be interrogated.

he pine tree shilling. The Roman umeral XII indicates the number of ence in a shilling.

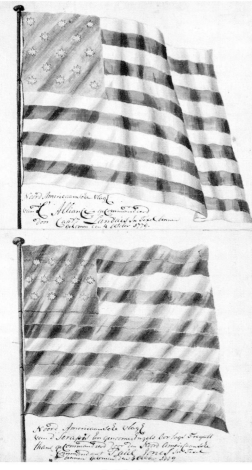

John Paul Jones' *Ranger* flew the first U.S. official flag in 1778, but a year later, these variations on the design were observed by a Dutch artist aboard Jones' *Alliance* (top) and *Serap.* (bottom). The design for the flag wasn't legally standardized until 1818 (Chicago Historical Society)

♦ 14 ♦

1627 Dutch settlers, who had tried to establish their own thriving colony on the Delaware River, give up and join Peter Minuit's settlement on Manhattan Island. **1777** The Continental Congress agrees to a national flag with thirteen stripes and thirteen white stars in a field of blue "representing the new constellation." **1846** In California a New England schoolteacher named William Ide leads eighteen men in an assault on a Sonoma military post and proclaims independence from Mexico in the name of the Bear Republic. Eleven days later John C. Frémont, representing the United States, arrives on the scene and on July 5 is named head of state. **1941** President Roosevelt freezes all German and Italian assets in the United States. **1951** Univac I, the first commercially built computer, goes into operation at the Census Bureau in Philadelphia.

✦ 15 ✦

1775 George Washington becomes supreme commander of the Continental Army. In a letter to Abigail Adams, John Adams describes him as "modest and virtuous . . . amiable, generous and brave." Washington is, for the time being, the entire army, since no other appointments or enlistments have been made. **1836** Arkansas becomes the twenty-fifth state of the Union. **1844** The inventor Charles Goodyear receives a patent for vulcanization, which prevents rubber from becoming sticky in warm weather. Goodyear's discovery is the result of an accidental spill of rubber on a stove. **1846** America's northwest border, disputed with Britain for some time, is resolved in the Oregon Treaty, which sets the boundary at the 49th parallel. "Fifty-four Forty or Fight" had been President Polk's campaign slogan, but this compromise is made peaceably. Once the treaty is announced, there is an enormous increase in the migration of Eastern Americans to the Oregon Territory.

✦ 16 ✦

1788 The Virginia convention, home of many opponents of the new Constitution, meets to discuss ratification. Patrick Henry, fearing that a strong central government would trample on the states and indignant at the lack of a Bill of Rights, is opposed. James Madison, who had much to do with creating the Constitution, is the principal defender. **1941** As relations with the Axis powers deteriorate, President Roosevelt orders the closing of all German and Italian consulates in the United States. Germany and Italy reciprocate on June 19.

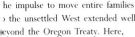

JUNE 15

The impulse to move entire families to the unsettled West extended well beyond the Oregon Treaty. Here, migrants of a later generation pause for a photograph near Colorado Springs. (Western History Department, Denver Public Library)

J O I N, or D I E.

JUNE 19
Benjamin Franklin expressed the argument for union graphically in his *Pennsylvania Gazette*. (Library of Congress)

✦ 17 ✦

1775 The Battle of Bunker Hill (actually Breed's Hill) is fought in Charlestown, outside Boston. The rebels fight well, and the British losses are heavy, including Major John Pitcairn, who is shot just after shouting, "The day is ours." The shot is credited to Peter Salem, who had recently been freed from slavery. **1947** Pan American Airways introduces around the world service for a fare of $1,700. **1963** The Supreme Court rules that it is unconstitutional to require Bible reading and the Lord's prayer in public schools. **1972** Five men are arrested for breaking into the offices of the Democratic National Committee at the Watergate Building in Washington. The men turn out to be employees of the Committee to Re-elect the President, or CREEP.

✦ 18 ✦

1787 Delegates to the Constitutional Convention are surprised when Alexander Hamilton of New York proposes that the nation's chief executive serve for life and have absolute veto power over legislation. "If Hamilton were now living," wrote John Quincy Adams fifty years later, "he would not dare, in an assembly of Americans, even with closed doors, to avow the opinions of this speech, or to present such a plan even as a speculation." **1886** At a meeting of the Association of American Physicians, Dr. Reginald Fitz offers a theory that many mysterious abdominal disorders are caused by a diseased appendix. He names the condition appendicitis, later remarking that he greatly preferred that name to "Fitz' disease." **1979** President Jimmy Carter and Chairman Leonid Brezhnev sign the SALT II agreement (Strategic Arms Limitation Treaty) limiting long-range missiles and bombers to 2,250 for each country.

✦ 19 ✦

1754 Six colonies send delegates to the Albany Congress in Albany, New York, to discuss ways to bring the colonies into closer cooperation. Thomas Hutchinson of Massachusetts and Benjamin Franklin of Pennsylvania submit plans, and in July the Congress arrives at a final proposal that calls for a union of all colonies except Georgia and Nova Scotia, with a president-general appointed by the king and a grand council of representatives from colonial assemblies. The plan is rejected by the colonial legislatures as well as the British government. **1846** The first recorded baseball game is played in Hoboken, New Jersey, following rules laid out by Alexander Cartwright. **1977** Bohemian-born Jon Nepomucene Neumann, who was bishop of Philadelphia from 1852 to 1860, is canonized by Pope Paul VI as the first American male saint.

✦ 20 ✦

1790 In a compromise it is decided the new federal capital should be on the Potomac in Virginia instead of Philadelphia. In exchange for this concession by the Northern states, James Madison agrees to solicit support in the South for a plan to have the federal government assume debts incurred by the individual states during the Revolution. **1863** West Virginia is admitted to the Union as the thirty-fifth state after breaking away from Confederate Virginia. **1864** Through poor coordination the Union forces miss an opportunity to take Petersburg from the Confederates and move on to Richmond. During a lull a private from Maine, John W. Haley, records the Union mood in his journal: "Nothing for excitement except that a few men were picked off by sharpshooters. A feeling prevails that sooner or later this experience will befall us all."

JUNE 20
"We have an indefinable dread, our nerves subjected to a continual strain which we know cannot end till the war ends, or we are wiped out," wrote Private Haley. Snipers at Petersburg, sketched by Alfred Waud. (Library of Congress)

✦ 21 ✦

1788 New Hampshire becomes the ninth state to ratify the new Constitution, satisfying Article VII of the document: "The Ratification of the Conventions of nine States, shall be sufficient for the Establishment of this Constitution between the states so ratifying the Same." Approval was not a foregone conclusion and required assiduous lobbying. **1834** Cyrus McCormick receives a patent for his improvement on the reaper, then sets about creating further improvements. His first reaper doesn't go on the market until 1841 and doesn't sell well until the 1850s, when it begins revolutionizing American agriculture. **1942** A Japanese submarine fires on the Oregon coast but causes no damage. **1945** After a two and one-half-month ordeal devastating to both sides, the Japanese surrender at Okinawa. The deaths number 12,500 on the American side, 160,000 on the Japanese. **1948** Columbia Records introduces the 33⅓ RPM long-playing record.

✦ 22 ✦

1750 Massachusetts minister Jonathan Edwards, who has resisted a liberalization of doctrine, is fired from his Northhampton church and moves to the colony's western frontier, where he has a small congregation of settlers and preaches to the local Indians. **1767** The *Boston Post Boy* advertises the services of Elizabeth Shaw, a shoemaker from London: "She undertakes to make and mend Men's Leather Shoes, in the Neatest Manner." **1775** The Second Continental Congress approves the fledgling nation's first issue of paper money. **1944** President Franklin D. Roosevelt signs the GI Bill, or, as it is formally known, the Servicemen's Readjustment Act. Instead of a lump sum bonus, as after World War I, this measure provides grants for specific purposes like housing and education.

✦ 23 ✦

1683 William Penn signs a treaty with the local Indians at Shackamaxon under the Treaty Elm. Penn would write of Pennsylvania's natives: "Their language is lofty, yet narrow, but like the Hebrew . . . one word serves in the place of three. . . . They are great concealers of their own resentments . . . but in liberality they excell, nothing is too good for their friend. . . . If they are ignorant of our pleasures, they are also free from our pains. . . . We sweat and toil to live; their pleasure feeds them;

JUNE 23
Remington's first typewriter advertisements were aimed at male professionals. (Smithsonian Institution)

INE 23
Quaker folk artist painted this
commemoration of William Penn's
meeting with the Delaware at
Shackamaxon. (Abby Aldrich Rockefeller Folk Art Center, Williamsburg,
Virginia)

I mean their hunting, fishing and fowling. . . . " **1810** The
Pacific Fur Company is established by German immigrant John
Jacob Astor, whose plan is to establish trading posts along the
route of the Lewis and Clark expedition. **1868** A patent for a
typewriter is awarded to Christopher Latham Sholes, who continues making improvements on the device and will sell the
patent in 1873 to E. Remington & Sons.

✦ 24 ✦

1497 Italian navigator John Cabot, sailing under the British
flag, sights land in the area of Cape Breton or Newfoundland
and claims it for Henry VII. He describes the coast as "swarm-
ing with fish." **1675** King Philip of the Wampanoags, the son
of the friendly chief Massasoit, leads a confederation of New
England tribes in a raid on the Plymouth colony. **1936** Mary
McLeod Bethune is appointed director of Negro affairs for the
National Youth Administration, the first black woman to hold a
major federal office.

A pictograph of Custer's last stand, painted in 1898 by Kicking Bear, a veteran of Little Big Horn. General Custer is dressed in buckskin at left center. The outline figures at upper left are departing spirits of combatants. Women of the Sioux village prepare a victory dance at lower right. (Southwest Museum, Los Angeles)

✦ 25 ✦

1788 Virginia ratifies the Constitution and becomes the tenth state of the Union. **1868** Congress passes a landmark law providing an eight-hour workday for "all laborers, workmen, and mechanics now employed or who may be employed by or on behalf of the Government of the United States." This proves difficult to enforce, however, when the Supreme Court rules that it does not apply to government contractors. **1876** Having reached the Indian camp at Little Big Horn, General Custer ignores scouting reports about the size of the enemy force, divides his 600 troops into three battalions, and orders one company of 112 to lead an attack. At least 2,000 Sioux and Cheyenne warriors overwhelm Custer's troops. A horse and a scout are the only Army survivors. **1941** President Roosevelt issues Executive Order 8802, which forbids discrimination based on race, creed, color or national origin in government and defense industries.

✦ 26 ✦

1721 Boston physician Zabdiel Boylston administers America's first smallpox inoculations, to his son and two slaves. Boylston learned of the procedure from Onesimus, a slave owned by Cotton Mather and an expert on African folk medicine. **1797** Charles Newbold receives a patent for a cast-iron plough. Farmers resist replacing their wooden ploughs, however, because they fear the new material will contaminate the soil. **1893** Financial panic follows a drop in the international trading value of the silver dollar from 67 cents to below 60 cents in gold. By the end of the year the nation's gold reserves have plummeted, 493 banks and over 15,000 businesses have failed. **1945** A charter for the new United Nations is approved in San Francisco by delegates from fifty countries.

✦ 27 ✦

1542 Navigator Juan Rodriguez Cabrillo sails up the coast of California as far north as Drake's Bay and claims the territory for Spain. **1831** Black Hawk, chief of the Sauk Indians of Illinois, agrees to move his people west of the Mississippi to accommodate white settlers on his tribal lands. The move is a failure, and when tribesmen attempt to recross the river to plant their traditional fields, they are attacked by settlers, beginning the Black Hawk War. **1841** The American whaler *John Howland* rescues five Japanese from a shipwreck. One of the five, a boy named Manjiro Nakahama, is brought back to New Bedford, Massachusetts, thus becoming the first Japanese immigrant to America. After several years he returned home and served as an interpreter during Commodore Perry's diplomatic mission in 1854. **1844** In Carthage, Illinois, a mob murders Joseph Smith, the founder of Mormonism. Attacks against the Mormons convince them that they must seek refuge in the unsettled West.

JUNE 30
President Theodore Roosevelt playe̶ a major role in pressuring the mea̶ packing industry to reform its way̶ (Culver Pictures)

✦ 28 ✦

1762 The *Boston Gazette* reports on an attempted counterfeiting: "Wednesday last a Man pretending to belong to Windsor of Hartford, in Connecticutt, made Application to some printers in Town to purchase a number of Printing Types, and afterwards to an Engraver, to cut him a Plate in imitation of the Money of that Colony, particularly 40s. Bills." **1852** Cholera is reported in New York City, the start of America's first cholera epidemic, spreading west and taking an especially heavy toll among the Indian tribes of the Great Plains. **1904** Helen Keller, blind and deaf, graduates with honors from Radcliffe College. Keller has already become a celebrity through the publication of her inspiring autobiography.

✦ 29 ✦

1620 Parliament prohibits the growing of tobacco in England, making it an exclusive import of the colonies, especially Virginia, whose exports rise from 20,000 pounds in 1618 to 500,000 pounds in 1627. By the 1680s, Virginia and Maryland together will be exporting about 28 million pounds a year. **1767** The British crown approves the Townshend Revenue Acts, promulgated by Chancellor of the Exchequer Charles "Champagne Charlie" Townshend to raise money in the colonies. Import taxes will be imposed on tea, glass, paint, oil, lead, and paper, among other items. **1970** The Supreme Court review of *Furman* v. *Georgia* concludes that the death penalty as formulated in Georgia and other states constitutes cruel and unusual punishment and therefore violates the Eighth Amendment.

✦ 30 ✦

1632 Cecilius Calvert, the second Lord Baltimore, is awarded proprietorship of Maryland, a new colony north of the Potomac River. The colony's charter leaves open the question of an official church, which makes it possible for Baltimore to establish a haven for his fellow Roman Catholics. **1808** Simeon North, a gunsmith who developed machinery for the manufacture of interchangeable parts, is awarded a Navy contract for boarding pistols. **1870** By a tie vote—28 to 28—the Senate blocks approval of a treaty to annex the Dominican Republic. **1906** Thanks in part to the influence of Upton Sinclair's novel *The Jungle,* Congress passes the Meat Inspection Act. And on the same day, thanks to the work of the Agriculture Department's research chemist Harvey W. Wiley, Congress also passes the Pure Food and Drugs Act. **1948** Bell Laboratories announces the development of the transistor as a substitute for radio tubes.

JUNE 28

The young Helen Keller. (S. M. Robson/Sophia Smith Collection, Smith College)

July

On Post in Camp,
First Half Hour

On Post in Camp,
Second half hour.

On Post in Camp
Third half hour

On Post in Camp
Last half hour!

JULY 20 (Opening illustration)
Earthrise photographed on the moon
by Apollo 11 astronauts. (National
Aeronautics and Space Administration)

JULY 1
On Post in Camp, from Whistler's
West Point years. (West Point Museum Collections, United States Mili
tary Academy)

JULY 20 (Opening illustration)
Earthrise photographed on the moon
by Apollo 11 astronauts. (National
Aeronautics and Space Administration)

JULY 1
On Post in Camp, from Whistler's
West Point years. (West Point Museum Collections, United States Mili
tary Academy)

✦ 1 ✦

1847 Congress authorizes the first issue of postage stamps.
Before this, mail had been paid for by the recipient, not the
sender. **1851** James McNeill Whistler enters West Point, a
misturn in the career of the future artist that ends when he is
discharged for incompetence in chemistry. "Had silicon been a
gas," he said, "I would have been a major general." **1904** The
Bureau of Entomology is founded under director L. O. Howard, famed for his studies of the housefly and malaria mos-
quito. **1950** The day after President Truman orders a naval
blockade of the Korean coast, United States forces enter the
Korean conflict. **1972** *Ms.* magazine begins publication.

JULY 2
Thomas Jefferson and his committee
present the Declaration of Independence to the Continental Congress;
detail of painting *The Declaration of
Independence* by John Trumbull. (©
Yale University Art Gallery)

✦ 2 ✦

1730 From the colonial annals of crime, the *Pennsylvania Gazette* reports on the doings of Alexander Cummings, "a most successful cheat," who swindled a number of South Carolina residents in a loan office fraud. **1776** The Continental Congress votes to declare independence from Britain. Thomas Jefferson presents the Declaration his committee has been working on, and debate begins. **1862** President Lincoln signs the Morrill Act, which offers each Union state public land to establish agricultural colleges. **1881** President Garfield is fatally shot in a Washington, D.C., railroad station by Charles J. Guiteau, a frustrated job seeker. **1964** President Johnson signs a landmark civil rights bill, passed after surviving a three-month filibuster, that forbids discrimination in voting, employment, and access to public places.

Bronzes cast from life masks of John Adams at the age of ninety and of Thomas Jefferson, both by John Browere. (New York State Historical Association, Cooperstown)

✦ 3 ✦

1852 In recognition of the impact of the Gold Rush, Congress approves the construction of a branch of the United States mint in San Francisco. **1863** On the third day of fighting at Gettysburg, Pennsylvania, General Lee makes a last desperate attempt to break the Union lines by a direct attack on Seminary Ridge. **1890** Idaho is admitted to the Union as the forty-third state. **1898** Four Spanish armored cruisers attempt to break the blockade at Santiago de Cuba and are fired upon by superior American battleships. Before the shooting stops, 600 Spanish sailors (and only one American) are killed. Captain John W. Philip calls to his crew aboard the USS *Texas:* "Don't cheer, men. The poor devils are dying."

✦ 4 ✦

1776 Delegates of twelve colonies ratify the Declaration of Independence. New York adds its late endorsement on July 9. **1826** At an Independence Day celebration in Washington, a collection is taken to help pay the debts of Thomas Jefferson. Later comes the news that he and his old adversary John Adams have both died on this day. **1831** Baptist Minister S. F. Smith introduces the song *America* to his congregation at Boston's Park Street Church. The words are by Smith, the tune from an old German song. **1951** A reporter for the *Madison* (Wisconsin) *Capital-Times* is rebuffed by 99 out of 100 people he asks to sign a petition made up of quotations from the Declaration of Independence and Bill of Rights. Many call the petition subversive.

JULY 7
Denied coverage in the conventional press, the Wobblies spread their message through posters and militant songs like *We Have Fed You All a Thousand Years,* with a text "by an unknown proletarian." (Industrial Workers of the World)

✦ 5 ✦

1653 Tensions heighten between English and Dutch settlers when England's Connecticut colony seizes the Dutch Fort Good Hope at Hartford. **1843** In the Oregon Territory, variously contested by Spain, Russia, and now most intensely by Britain and the United States, American migrants meet at Champoeg, a few miles south of modern Portland, to adopt a constitution modeled on that of Iowa. A provisional government is created on the understanding that as soon as possible the United States will extend its jurisdiction.

✦ 6 ✦

1699 New York businessman-turned-pirate Captain William Kidd is captured in Boston and sent to England for trial. **1776** The Declaration of Independence is announced on the front page of the *Pennsylvania Evening Gazette.* **1785** President Thomas Jefferson proposes a monetary decimal system with four coins: a ten dollar gold piece, silver dollar, silver dime, and copper penny. **1854** At a meeting of the new antislavery political party in Jackson, Michigan, the name Republican is chosen, with a deliberate reference to Thomas Jefferson's old Democratic-Republican Party. **1954** Elvis Presley, a self-taught nineteen-year-old singer, makes his first record, a combination of country music on one side and black rhythm and blues on the other that portends a revolution in popular music.

✦ 7 ✦

1775 Jacob Duché, the Anglican chaplain to the Continental Army, delivers a sermon in Philadelphia in support of the Revolution, "The Duty of Standing Fast in Our Spiritual and Temporal Liberties." But when the British enter the city, Duché will transfer his allegiance and later flee to England. **1865** Four people convicted of conspiring in the assassination of Abraham Lincoln are hanged in Washington, D.C. **1906** The Industrial Workers of the World, soon known as Wobblies, organize a left-wing alternative to the relatively staid American Federation of Labor. "The working class and the employing class have nothing in common," their constitution reads. "It is the historic mission of the working class to do away with capitalism."

✦ **8** ✦

1654 Jacob Barsimon, the first known Jew to settle in North America, arrives in Manhattan. Twenty-three more Jews reach the colonies this year. **1775** John Dickinson's Olive Branch Petition, signed by conservative members of the Continental Congress, is sent to King George III in the hope he will intervene to resolve the Americans' grievances. There is no reply from the king. **1835** The Liberty Bell cracks while tolling for the death of Supreme Court Chief Justice John Marshall. **1853** Commodore Matthew Perry leads a naval fleet of intimidating size into Japan's Yedo Bay. Perry's mission is to induce Japan to open trading relations with the United States, as much through a show of force as diplomacy. **1889** In the nation's last bare-knuckled championship boxing match, John L. Sullivan defeats Jake Kilrain after seventy-five rounds.

JLY 8
are Knuckles by George A. Hayes.
National Gallery of Art, Gift of Wil-
am and Bernice Chrysler Garbisch)

✦ 9 ✦

1755 General Edward Braddock, commander in chief of the British forces in North America, is ambushed by French and Indians on the Monongahela River near Fort Duquesne. When Braddock is mortally wounded, his civilian aide, twenty-three-year-old George Washington, leads the troops back to Fort Cumberland, Maryland. **1892** Pennsylvania state troopers are brought into Andrew Carnegie's Homestead steel mill, where striking workers had driven off Pinkerton agents hired by the plant manager, Henry Clay Frick. **1893** Black surgeon Dr. Daniel Hale Williams performs the world's first successful surgical closure of a heart wound in Chicago. Dr. Williams also helped organize the nation's first training school for black nurses. **1896** At the Democratic National Convention in Chicago, party leader William Jennings Bryan overwhelms the audience with his Cross of Gold speech, an emotional condemnation of the gold standard and its backers, the Republicans. The speech helps win Bryan the presidential nomination, although he is defeated by William McKinley in the fall.

✦ 10 ✦

1660 The Andover, Massachusetts, home of New England's first published poet, Ann Bradstreet, catches fire and is destroyed; "My pleasant things in ashes lie/And them behold no more shall I/Under that roof no guest shall sit,/Nor at thy table eat a bit." **1775** Horatio Gates, General Washington's adjutant general, issues an order excluding blacks from serving in the Continental Army. The order is reversed after Lord Dunmore, the deposed royal governor of Virginia, pledges freedom to all slaves who join the British. **1890** Wyoming is admitted to the Union as the forty-fourth state. **1943** American and British troops launch a successful five-week air and sea conquest of Sicily that leads to the invasion of Italy.

✦ 11 ✦

1767 John Quincy Adams, sixth President of the United States, is born in Braintree, Massachusetts, in a farmhouse where his father, future president John Adams, practices country law. **1794** On his twenty-eighth birthday Secretary of State John Quincy Adams joins President Washington at a meeting with a delegation of Chickasaw Indians. The president produced a peace pipe; Adams writes: "These Indians appeared to be quite unused to it, and from their manner of going through it, looked as if they were submitting to a process in compliance with *our* custom." **1804** Aaron Burr and Alexander Hamilton meet to resolve their differences in a duel in Weehawken, New Jersey, across the Hudson from Manhattan. **1941** President Franklin D. Roosevelt appoints William "Wild Bill" Donovan as his coordinator of defense information, with special responsibility to create a civilian intelligence agency, later called the OSS (Office of Strategic Services).

✦ 12 ✦

1808 The *Missouri Gazette,* the first newspaper west of the Mississippi, begins publication in St. Louis. **1817** The Boston *Columbian Sentinel* describes the presidency of James Monroe as the "era of good feeling," a label that sticks. It was the first time in about twenty-five years that the nation's political life hadn't been dominated by party feuding. **1909** Congress approves the Sixteenth Amendment, which gives the federal government the power to tax incomes.

JULY 9
The National Guard patrols near its encampment above the company town of Homestead after strikers forced 300 Pinkerton agents to surrender. (Library of Congress)

✦ 13 ✦

1658 The Massachusetts Bay Colony proceeds in a piece-by-piece annexation of Maine by taking Casco Bay. **1832** Geologist Henry R. Schoolcraft, author of pathbreaking field studies of Indian life, leads an expedition up the Mississippi and discovers its source at Lake Itasca, Minnesota. **1863** Rioting breaks out over the nation's first military draft, most violently in New York. Troops just back from Gettysburg must be called in to restore order. **1869** While rioting against Chinese immigrants occurs in San Francisco, where coolie labor is seen as a threat to white men's jobs, Memphis, Tennessee, is host to a convention that invites Chinese workers to settle in the South.

JULY 13
Schoolcraft landing at Lake Itasca, detail of an undated chromolithograph by Seth Eastman. (Minnesota Historical Society Art Collection)

✦ 14 ✦

1735 The *New York Gazette* advertises that at "The Sign of the black Horse in Smith street, near the old Dutch Church, is carefully taught the French and Spanish Languages, after the best Method that is now practised in Great Britain." **1790** The first anniversary of Bastille Day is celebrated in Philadelphia and elsewhere as a gesture of solidarity with Revolutionary France. **1881** William H. Bonney, known as Billy the Kid, is shot dead on his second jailbreak by Sheriff Pat Garrett at Fort Sumner, New Mexico. **1892** Civil War veterans wounded in service are granted a $50 monthly pension. A few weeks later women nurses who served in the war are granted a $12 monthly pension. **1913** Gerald R. Ford, the first president to take office under the Twenty-fifth Amendment and the first never to be elected president or vice president, is born in Omaha.

JULY 16
Father Junípero Serra. (Culver Pictures)

ULY 13
The New York draft riots soon turned to race riots as a Negro orphanage was burned and innocent blacks lynched. (New-York Historical Society)

✦ 15 ✦

1788 The Confederation Congress appoints Revolutionary War General Arthur St. Clair governor of the Ohio Territory, its last major achievement before being replaced by the Senate and House of Representatives. **1915** A scandal erupts when a Secret Service agent carries off a briefcase left on the New York subway by a German diplomat. Inside are documents that reveal the existence of a network of spies operating across the United States, which at this point is officially neutral in the Great War. **1971** President Richard Nixon accepts "with pleasure" an invitation to visit mainland China. It is understood the visit will lead to diplomatic recognition.

✦ 16 ✦

1769 Franciscan missionary Father Junípero Serra founds San Diego de Alcala, the first mission in upper California and first of a series built by the Franciscans. **1934** To protest police violence against the Maritime Union, San Francisco workers call for a general strike. Public transportation shuts down, as do most theaters and stores, and signs appear in store windows reading "Closed Till the Boys Win." The strike ends after three days when both sides accept government arbitration. **1936** Father Charles Coughlin, the anti-Semitic radio priest whose broadcasts have attracted a following of New Deal haters, is cheered when he calls the president a "great betrayer and liar" at a convention of supporters of the Townsend Plan, a scheme to end the Depression by giving monthly payments of $200 to everyone over sixty. **1945** The first atomic bomb is exploded in a test at Alamogordo, New Mexico.

✦ 17 ✦

1754 Reverend Samuel Johnson of Connecticut, first president of King's College in New York City—later named Columbia—welcomes the first class of eight students in a schoolhouse contributed by Trinity Church. **1775** The Continental Congress agrees to open a military hospital, in effect creating an Army medical department. **1821** The United States gains possession of Florida, which had been claimed by Spain since the explorations of Ponce de Leon, then passed to Britain, and returned to Spain after the United States won independence. **1948** Southern Democrats break from the national party to form the States Rights Party, or the Dixiecrats, and nominate Strom Thurmond of South Carolina to run for president.

✦ 18 ✦

1768 *The Liberty Song,* probably the first patriotic American song, appears in the *Boston Gazette* and goes on sale as a pamphlet. **1858** The Pennsylvania Railroad, making its first through-run from Philadelphia to Pittsburgh, introduces the first smoking car. **1918** Over a quarter million American soldiers begin the Aisne-Marne offensive, which by August 6 drives the Germans back along the Vesle River, a major turning point for the Allies. **1940** The VS-300 test helicopter designed by Russian immigrant Igor Sikorsky stays aloft for fifteen minutes in a test at Stratford, Connecticut. **1955** Disneyland, a vast theme park celebration of nostalgia and fantasy, opens in Anaheim, California.

JULY 20
Sitting Bull and family, photographed in 1881. (Library of Congress)

Igor Sikorsky at the controls in a test of his prototype helicopter. (UPI/Bettmann Newsphotos)

JULY 19
Elizabeth Cady Stanton. (Women's Rights National Historical Park)

✦ 19 ✦

1848 At the Seneca Falls, New York, home of Mrs. Elizabeth Cady Stanton, the first Women's Rights Convention meets. The published Declaration of Sentiments states: "We hold these truths to be self-evident; that all men *and women* are created equal. . . . The history of mankind is a history of repeated injuries and usurpations on the part of man toward woman, having in direct object the establishment of tyranny over her." The document is signed by the thirty-two men who attend, who include Frederick Douglass, and the sixty-eight women, who include Charlotte Woodward Pierce, who lived to vote in the presidential election of 1920. **1984** Geraldine Ferraro, congresswoman from Queens, New York, is nominated to run for vice president of the United States on the Democratic Party ticket, the first woman to be so nominated by a major party. **1985** NASA selects schoolteacher Christa McAuliffe from among 11,000 applicants to join the space shuttle.

✦ 20 ✦

1881 Chief Sitting Bull of the Sioux returns from exile in Canada to give himself up to U.S. authorities. Handing his rifle to his son, the conqueror of General Custer declares, "I wish it to be remembered that I was the last man of my tribe to surrender my rifle." **1969** Descending the steps of the lunar module *Eagle,* Neil A. Armstrong becomes the first man to set foot on the moon. With module pilot Edwin E. "Buzz" Aldrin, Armstrong leaves a plaque that reads: "Here men from the planet Earth first set foot upon the moon July, 1969, A.D. We came in peace for all mankind."

✦ 21 ✦

1861 The Battle of Bull Run, the first major encounter of the Civil War, brings together the inexperienced troops of both sides at Manassas, Virginia. The Union seems to prevail until Confederate reinforcements under General Thomas J. Jackson turn the tide for the rebels. Jackson earns the name "Stonewall" for his efforts. **1959** Judge Frederick van Pelt Bryan rules that *Lady Chatterly's Lover* can be legally sent through the mails: "To exclude this book from the mails on the grounds of obscenity would fashion a rule which could be applied to a substantial portion of the classics of our literature. Such a rule would be inimical to a free society."

✦ 22 ✦

1587 Explorer John White leads an expedition to the Roanoke, Virginia, colony founded by Sir Walter Raleigh. White finds no survivors but leaves a group of settlers and returns to England for supplies. When he returns August 17, 1590, the settlers are gone. The letters CRO carved on a tree and CROATOAN on a doorpost suggest the name of a nearby island, but no traces of the colonists could be found. **1934** John Dillinger, Public Enemy No. 1, is shot dead by the FBI outside a Chicago movie theater. **1948** Breakaway left-leaning Democrats form the Progressive Party and select former Vice President Henry Wallace to run against Harry Truman.

✦ 23 ✦

1766 America's oldest medical society is created during a meeting at Duff's Tavern in New Brunswick, New Jersey. The group's attempt to establish uniform fees and establish a licensing system for practitioners would not be successful. **1807** An ad in the *New Orleans Gazette* offers horse-drawn tow service up the Mississippi to Louisville for flatboat traders who had come downriver and completed their business. **1827** America's first swimming school opens in Boston, with former President John Quincy Adams as one of the students. **1846** In Concord, Massachusetts, Henry David Thoreau is arrested for refusing to pay a poll tax in protest against the Mexican War. Out of the experience comes his essay "Civil Disobedience." **1851** The Sioux tribes of the Midwest agree to give up most of their land in Iowa and Minnesota to the federal government and are confined to a strip of land along the upper Minnesota River.

✦ 24 ✦

1651 Anthony Johnson, a free black and former indentured servant, is granted 250 acres in Northampton County, Virginia. In following years Johnson and his relatives found a black community on the shores of the Pungoteague River. **1701** Antoine de la Mothe Cadillac arrives at the site of Detroit after a forty-nine-day canoe trip from Quebec. With him to found a fort and trading post are fifty soldiers, fifty settlers, and two priests. **1847** Brigham Young and his 143 Mormon followers, in search of a refuge from persecution in the East, reach the Great Salt Lake Basin, and Young declares, "This is the place."

_Y 23_

oreau at the age of thirty-seven,
essed for travel in a sketch by
_ friend D. Ricketson. (Bettmann_
chive)

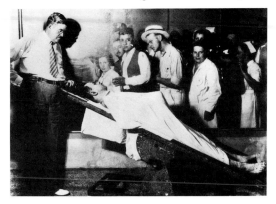

_Y 22_

n Dillinger's corpse became a
urist attraction at the Chicago
rgue, the culmination of a public-
campaign that helped popularize
_ e FBI and its young director,_
Edgar Hoover. (UPI/Bettmann
wsphotos)

✦ 25 ✦

1814 The bloodiest battle of the War of 1812 takes place at Lundy's Lane near Niagara Falls, where 2,600 Americans are overcome by a slightly larger British force and after five hours of combat retreat to Lake Erie. Each side suffers about 800 casualties. **1868** The Wyoming Territory is created out of portions of the Dakota, Idaho, and Utah territories on land which has primarily served as a route to the West. **1940** The United States bans the export of such critical war materials as oil and metal products, creating immediate shortages in Japan, where it is interpreted as being directed primarily against the Japanese. **1952** Puerto Rico adopts a new constitution which gives it the status of an autonomous commonwealth, voluntarily linked to the United States.

✦ 26 ✦

1775 The U.S. Post Office is established with Benjamin Franklin as postmaster. The year before the British had dismissed Franklin as copostmaster of the colonies because of his political activities. **1788** After much hesitation and debate New York ratifies the Constitution by a vote of 30–27 and becomes the eleventh state. **1947** Congress passes the National Security Act, which unifies the armed forces under the direction of a civilian secretary of defense, who will be a cabinet officer, and creates the National Security Council. **1948** By executive order President Harry S. Truman bars racial segregation in the armed forces and calls for an end to discrimination in federal employment.

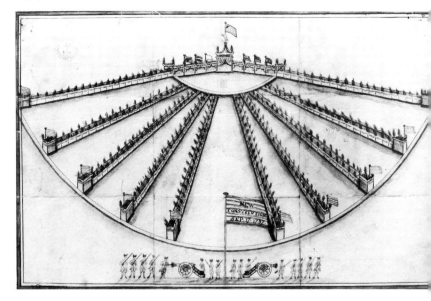

his lithograph commemorates the rrival of the Atlantic Cable in New-undland, an event that caused so uch excitement, diarist Philip Hone omplained, that people were calling "the greatest human achievement history." (Bettmann Archive)

✦ 27 ✦

1661 Parliament confirms the Navigation Act, which serves as a stimulus to the shipbuilding industry in America, where wood is plentiful and cheaper than in England. **1861** After the Union fiasco at Bull Run, command of the Federal Division is taken away from General McDowell and given to General McClellan, who once said, "I think there is scarcely a man in this whole army who would not give his life for me." **1867** A permanent telegraph cable spanning the Atlantic is completed after several unsuccessful attempts and one, in 1858, that failed after a few weeks. **1953** The Korean War formally ends with an armistice signed at Panmunjon, South Korea.

✦ 28 ✦

1849 Diarist Philip Hone reports on one of the perils of city life in the nineteenth century, cholera outbreaks: "Poor New York has become a charnel house; people die daily of cholera to the number of two or three hundred." **1868** A treaty between the United States and China is negotiated by former ambassador Anson Burlingame, who also designed for the flagless Chinese the imperial flag. **1868** The Fourteenth Amendment to the Constitution is ratified, guaranteeing the right to vote and equal protection under the laws to all citizens except women, whom it deliberately excludes.

he banquet pavilion to celebrate ew York's ratification, designed by erre Charles L'Enfant, who later ew the plan for the new capital ty of Washington. (New-York His-rical Society)

✦ 29 ✦

1676 Sir William Berkeley, royal governor of Virginia, moves to subdue a rebellion in the colony by outlawing its leader, Nathaniel Bacon, but opposition continues to the placatory Indian policies that triggered the rebellion, and the governor is eventually driven out of Jamestown. The rebellion subsides with the sudden death of Bacon. **1858** Townsend Harris, the American consul to Japan, completes a new trade agreement that allows Americans to take up residence anywhere in Japan, a privilege hitherto denied to outsiders. **1888** An epidemic of yellow fever breaks out in Jacksonville, Florida, and ravages the region for most of the remaining year. **1928** The iron lung electric respirator, invented by Dr. Phillip Drinker and Dr. Louis A. Shaw, is put into use at Bellevue Hospital in New York City.

✦ 30 ✦

1740 Caspar Wistar, a manufacturer of brass buttons, opens a glass factory near Salem, New Jersey. Wistar specializes in windows, made in "common sizes" or to order, and bottles and at the suggestion of Benjamin Franklin later adds Leyden jars for scientific experimentation. **1965** Over the objections of the American Medical Association, the Social Security Act is amended to create Medicare, a government-funded health insurance plan for the elderly. **1975** Jimmy Hoffa, former head of the Teamsters Union, is seen in public for the last time.

JULY 30
Four examples of eighteenth-century New Jersey glassmaking. The free-blown candlesticks and sugar bowl may have been made at Caspar Wistar's factory. (Corning Museum of Glass, Corning, New York)

neral Grant, at left, on Lookout
untain, 1863. (National Archives)

✦ 31 ✦

1619 Virginia's House of Burgesses, the first legislature in the colonies, proposes that wives should be given shares of land in the Jamestown community "because that in a plantation it is not known whether man or woman be the most necessary." **1790** The first American patent is awarded to Samuel Hopkins of Vermont, who has invented an improved method of making potash. **1861** President Lincoln appoints Army dropout Ulysses Grant a general of volunteers in the Union Army, something of an honorary appointment in most cases but in Grant's a step in the rehabilitation of his career. **1874** Patrick Francis Healy, a Jesuit, is inaugurated as president of Georgetown University in Washington, D.C. Healy is the first black to head a predominantly white university.

August

✦ 1 ✦

1870 The Utah Territory allows women to vote in local elections. But pending in the U.S. Congress is a law that would disenfranchise them unless the state abolished polygamy. The law passes, and Utah women do not vote again until 1896, when the Mormon Church renounces plural marriage and Utah gains statehood. **1876** Colorado is admitted to the Union as the thirty-eighth state. **1903** A Packard completes the first cross-country auto trip, covering the distance from San Francisco to New York in fifty-two days. **1933** The Blue Eagle appears as the symbol of the National Recovery Administration (NRA), President Roosevelt's attempt to pressure the business community to regulate itself. **1946** The Atomic Energy Commission is established to promote peaceful uses of atomic energy.

✦ 2 ✦

1776 Copies of the Declaration of Independence arrive from the copyist, and the delegates to the Continental Congress inscribe their names. The first to sign, John Hancock, writes in large letters, declaring, "There, King George will be able to read that without his spectacles." **1861** A national income tax bill is passed to help finance the Union war effort. By 1865 the income tax produces 20 percent of federal income, as against 23 percent for manufacturing and sales taxes. The cost of the war is far greater than the income potential of the tax system, however, and most of the expenses are borne by loans and

AUGUST 26 *(Opening illustration)*
Members of the National Woman's Party celebrate the vote at their headquarters in Washington, D.C. (Library of Congress)

AUGUST 1
8,000 children rally for the NRA in San Francisco. (UPI/Bettmann Newsphotos)

AUGUST 3

In this 1893 cartoon from *Puck* descendants of immigrants bar the way to newcomers. (Smithsonian Institution)

issues of paper money. **1920** Marcus Garvey, leader of the Universal Improvement Association, a black nationalist movement, calls on 25,000 followers at Madison Square Garden in New York City to work toward economic self-sufficiency and a return to Africa.

✦ **3** ✦

1492 Navigator Christopher Columbus, probably of Genoese origin but sailing in the service of Spain, embarks from Palos, Spain, one half hour before sunrise, in search of a western route to the Orient. **1842** Diarist Philip Hone reports after a trip to the countryside that he "frequently heard used the word 'dickering,' which until then was new to me. It means 'barter' and is an expression indicating the signs of the times. The valleys . . . stand thick with corn, but . . . there is no money in circulation, and the farmer is compelled to 'dicker' his wheat for molasses and tea and sugar, his wool for broadcloths, and must part with a horse or an ox to get fodder for the rest of his stock." **1882** Congress passes the first law to restrict immigration, imposing a 50 cent tax on all new arrivals and barring the way to paupers, convicts, and people judged physically or mentally defective.

✦ **4** ✦

1735 In a triumph for freedom of the press, German immigrant newspaperman John Peter Zenger is acquitted of the charge of seditious libel. The gadfly editor of New York's *Weekly Journal* had tormented the governor and his cronies with relentless satire, but the state was unable to convince a jury that Zenger's writing was a crime. **1892** Andrew Borden, a prosperous merchant in Fall River, Massachusetts, and his second wife, Abby, are murdered at home by someone wielding a hatchet. Andrew's daughter, Lizzie, will be brought to trial for the killings and acquitted. **1922** The 13 million telephones in America observe a minute's silence in memory of their inventor, Alexander Graham Bell, whose funeral is today.

✦ 5 ✦

1583 Sir Humphrey Gilbert, leading an underfunded expedition to the New World, founds England's first North American colony at St. Johns, Newfoundland. On the return voyage Gilbert's party runs into a storm and all are drowned. **1884** On Bedloe's Island in New York harbor, the cornerstone is laid for a 151-foot-high pedestal on which the Statue of Liberty, a French gift to the United States, will rest. **1914** The first American traffic light is installed at the intersection of Euclid Avenue and East 105th Street in Cleveland. **1964** While American planes attack North Vietnamese bases and PT boats in retaliation for an attack on two U.S. destroyers in the Gulf of Tonkin, President Lyndon Johnson's aides present a resolution to Senate Foreign Relations Committee chairman William Fulbright that empowers the president to use military force in Vietnam without declaring war.

✦ 6 ✦

1774 "Mother Ann" Lee arrives in America from England to found a religious celibate community known as the Shakers. **1777** Both sides claim victory in the Revolutionary War Battle of Oriskany, in which Mohawk Chief Joseph Brant led a combined force of Indians and Tories in the attack on American troops along the Mohawk River in upstate New York. Dartmouth-educated Brant is the brother in-law of the late Sir William Johnson, who had been King George's superintendent of Indian affairs. **1801** A rousing Presbyterian camp meeting in Cane Ridge, Kentucky, marks the beginning of the Second Great Awakening or Great Revival of the West. **1945** The

AUGUST 5

Ceremonial trowel for the cornerstone of the Liberty pedestal, whose financing depended on a difficult public fund-raising campaign. (Geneseo Lodge #214, Free and Accepted Order of Masons, New York)

AUGUST 8

Shoshoni Indians welcome President Arthur. The umbrellas are leadership symbols. (F. Jay Haynes/Montana Historical Society, Helena)

B-29 Superfortress bomber *Enola Gay* drops an atomic bomb on Hiroshima. About 80,000 of the city's 343,000 people are killed, and another 200,000 are injured.

✦ **7** ✦

1673 Dutch ships bombard the English garrison on Manhattan Island, which surrenders five days later and remains under Dutch control for several months. **1782** General Washington establishes the Badge of Military Merit, or Purple Heart, to honor wounded soldiers. The award is discontinued after the Revolution but revived in 1932. **1942** In an attempt to begin the reconquest of the Pacific, U.S. forces land on Guadalcanal in the Solomon Islands, meeting light resistance at first. **1959** The U.S. satellite *Explorer VI* sends back the first photograph of Earth taken from space.

✦ **8** ✦

1829 The Stourbridge Lion, built in Britain but the first steam-powered locomotive to operate in the United States, runs at ten miles per hour between Carbondale and Honesdale, Pennsylvania. But after this demonstration the Delaware & Hudson resumes the use of horses to pull coal trains over its tracks. **1883** In the first official visit by an American president to the Indians of the West, Shoshoni Chief Washakie receives Chester A. Arthur at the Wind River Reservation in Wyoming. **1942** President Franklin D. Roosevelt and British Prime Minister Winston Churchill agree that General Dwight D. Eisenhower should command the Allied invasion of North Africa.

AUGUST 6

Barn dance at a nineteenth-century Shaker commune in New York. (The Huntington Library, San Marino, California)

✦ 9 ✦

1842 Secretary of State Daniel Webster and Britain's Lord Ashburton conclude the Webster-Ashburton Treaty, which fixes the disputed U.S.-Canadian border along the states of New York, Vermont, and Maine. Border arguments between Maine and New Brunswick nearly led to war in 1839. **1936** At the Olympic Games in Berlin, which host Adolf Hitler had planned as a showcase for the achievements of the Nazi regime, America's Jesse Owens steals the limelight by winning four gold medals in track. **1945** After cloud cover obscures the intended target, Nagasaki becomes the target of Fat Man, the second atom bomb dropped over Japan. **1974** President Richard M. Nixon, under threat of impeachment for lying to conceal his role in the cover-up of the Watergate burglary, resigns.

✦ 10 ✦

1821 Missouri, the second state to be created from the Louisiana Purchase, is admitted to the Union as the twenty-fourth state. **1835** A mob in Canaan, New Hampshire, sets fire to the Noyes Academy after fourteen black students enroll. **1846** The Smithsonian Institution is established from a bequest by James Smithson, the wealthy illegitimate son of the Duke of Northumberland. Smithson, a chemist and mineralogist, had never visited the United States and the reason for the bequest is unknown. **1874** Herbert Clark Hoover, thirty-first president of the United States, is born in West Branch, Iowa. **1945** Japan indicates it would be willing to surrender if Emperor Hirohito can keep his throne.

✦ 11 ✦

1834 In the Charlestown section of Boston, hostility to Irish Catholic immigrants is fueled by a rumor that a young woman is being held against her will in an Ursuline convent. At night a mob breaks into the convent to liberate the supposed prisoner and then sets fire to the building. **1841** Runaway slave Frederick Douglass speaks in public for the first time, at an antislavery conference on Nantucket Island. "It was a severe cross, and I took it up reluctantly," he wrote later. "The truth was, I felt myself a slave, and the idea of speaking to white people weighed me down." **1965** A protest against police brutality in the Watts ghetto of Los Angeles, where male unemployment is estimated at 30 percent, triggers other resentments and turns into widespread looting and property destruction that continue for several days.

An assembly line at Isaac Singer's sewing machine factory in the late 1850s. (M. B. Schnapper)

Frederick Douglass gained freedom by borrowing the identity papers of a free black. As a former slave, he was a spellbinding witness to the evils of slavery. (Private collection)

✦ 12 ✦

1809 Shawnee Chief Tecumseh, who has organized a confederacy to resist the westward push of settlers, begins a series of fruitless meetings with the governor of Indian Territory, William Henry Harrison. Harrison calls Tecumseh a "Moses" but refuses to grant concessions. **1851** Isaac M. Singer receives a patent for the first continuous-stitch sewing machine. Singer is hit with protracted and successful lawsuits brought by Elias Howe, inventor of the first sewing machine. Nevertheless, so successful is Singer's machine, which has many improvements over Howe's, that the penalty payments are soon recovered, and business booms. **1945** Edward R. Murrow, whose wartime radio broadcasts from Europe gave many Americans their most immediate sense of World War II, speaks of the mood in Europe now that it is over: "Seldom, if ever, has a war ended leaving the victors with such a sense of uncertainty and fear, with such a realization that the future is obscure and that survival is not assured."

AUGUST 13

"And ever, as we go, there is some new pinnacle or tower, some crag or peak, some distant view of the upper plateau, some strange shaped rock, or some deep, narrow side canyon." *The Chasm of The Colorado* by Thomas Moran, whom Powell brought to the Grand Canyon some years later. (National Museum of American Art, Smithsonian Institution/U.S. Department of the Interior)

✦ 13 ✦

1680 The New Mexico Indians drive their Spanish rulers out of Sante Fe, which leads to a bitter war of reconquest that lasts ten years. **1870** John Wesley Powell, the first white explorer of the Grand Canyon, records his impressions: "We are now ready to start on our way down the Great Unknown. . . . We are three quarters of a mile in the depths of the earth, and the great river shrinks into insignificance. . . . We have an unknown distance yet to run; an unknown river yet to explore. What falls there are, we know not; what rocks beset the channel, we know not; what walls rise over the river, we know not. Ah, well! we may conjecture many things. The men talk as cheerfully as ever; jests are bandied about freely this morning; but to me the cheer is somber and the jests are ghastly."

✦ 14 ✦

1870 John Wesley Powell continues his exploration of the unknown in the Grand Canyon: "The walls, now, are more than a mile in height. . . . A thousand feet of this is up through granite crags, then steep slopes and perpendicular cliffs rise, one above another, to the summit. . . . Down in these grand, gloomy depths we glide, ever listening, for the mad waters keep up their roar; ever watching, ever peering ahead, for the narrow canyon is winding; and the river is closed in so that we can see but a few hundred yards, and what there may be below we know not. . . . And ever, as we go, there is some new pinnacle or tower, some crag or peak, some distant view of the upper plateau, some strange shaped rock or some deep, narrow side canyon." **1935** President Roosevelt signs the Social Security Act, the nation's first system of retirement income.

✦ 15 ✦

1790 Father John Carroll is consecrated as America's first Roman Catholic bishop. He is the founder of Georgetown University and a cousin to Charles Carroll, the only Catholic signer of the Declaration of Independence. **1846** California's first newspaper, *Californian,* begins publication in Monterey, two days before Americans, who have seized power from the local Spanish representatives, declare California an American territory. **1914** A deranged servant sets fire to Taliesen, the Wisconsin home of Frank Lloyd Wright, which embodies his visionary architectural principles.

✦ 16 ✦

1777 At the Battle of Bennington in Vermont, General John Stark leads his men up against the mercenaries of General Burgoyne: "My men, yonder are the Hessians. They were bought for seven pounds and ten pence a man. Are you worth more? Prove it. Tonight, the American flag floats from yonder hill or Molly Stark sleeps a widow!" **1858** Queen Victoria and President James Buchanan exchange greetings by telegraph to celebrate the laying of the transatlantic cable, which was completed August 6 but breaks down after a few weeks. **1896** Gold is discovered on Klondike Creek in the Yukon Territory, Canada. **1916** The United States and Canada sign a treaty to protect migratory birds.

AUGUST 17
The Cincinnati *Public Landing* by John C. Wild (1835), a view of the prospering city on the Ohio River. (Cincinnati Historical Society)

AUGUST 16
A new Gold Rush brought thousands of people into the Yukon, including entire families. (Special Collections Division, University of Washington Libraries)

✦ 17 ✦

1788 The town of Losantville in the Ohio Territory is founded by a land speculator and settlers from New Jersey. The following year it is renamed Cincinnati, in honor of the hereditary Society of the Cincinnati, formed by a group of Washington's veteran officers. **1807** The *Clermont,* a small steamboat designed by Robert Fulton, departs New York City for a five-mile-an-hour, thirty-two-hour trip up the Hudson to Albany. Thanks to a monopoly granted by the state of New York, Fulton demonstrates that steamboat operation can be profitable. **1915** In Marietta, Georgia, Leo Frank, a factory owner serving a life term for the murder of an employee, is taken from his jail cell by townspeople and lynched. Frank, a Jew who had moved south from New York, is widely perceived to be a victim of prejudice. In 1986, after considering new evidence, the state of Georgia issued a posthumous pardon. **1942** A raid over Rouen, France, is the first European bombing run undertaken exclusively by U.S. forces.

✦ 18 ✦

1587 Virginia Dare is born in Roanoke to Eleanor White Dare and Ananias Dare. The first English child born in the New World, she will disappear into history, like the other inhabitants of the Roanoke colony. **1873** John Lucas, Charles D. Begole, and A. H. Johnson become the first climbers to reach the top of Mount Whitney, highest peak in the lower forty-eight states. **1969** After three days of rock music, celebration, and invocation of the spirit of the decade, the Woodstock Festival ends in upstate New York.

✦ 19 ✦

1768 Workers revolt in the new colony of New Smyrna, Florida, whose 1,400 settlers from Minorca, Leghorn, and Greece are the second largest mass migration in the colonies. **1812** In a battle off Nova Scotia the U.S.S. *Constitution* sinks H.M.S. *Guerrière* in half an hour, raising national morale after the surrender of Detroit and a massacre at Fort Dearborn, the site of Chicago. Among the crew of the *Constitution* is Lucy Brewster, who served three years under the name Nicholas Baker. **1856** Surveyor and farmer Gail Borden patents his process for condensing milk. Introduced during the Civil War and then popularized by returning soldiers, condensed milk becomes the basis for a new processed food industry. **1914** As war breaks out across Europe, President Woodrow Wilson proclaims America's intention to remain neutral.

✦ 20 ✦

1636 Roger Williams draws up a covenant for his new settlement, Providence Plantations. It pledges that the majority will rule "only in civill things," leaving liberty of conscience to the individual. **1833** Benjamin Harrison, twenty-third president of the United States, is born in North Bend, Ohio, the grandson of President William Henry Harrison. Harrison "would never

AUGUST 18
Yasgur's Farm, Woodstock, New York, during the rock festival.
(© Baron Wolman)

know," the chairman of the Republican National Committee once said, "how close a number of men were compelled to approach the penitentiary in order to make him president." **1912** The Plant Quarantine Act comes into effect, placing restrictions on the entry of plants into the United States.

✦ 21 ✦

1874 An adultery suit is brought against Henry Ward Beecher of Brooklyn, a celebrated minister whose preaching helped bridge the gap between the old Puritan tenets and the new age. Beecher, the brother of Harriet Beecher Stowe, is acquitted in court and a special church hearing, but the case attracts notoriety to the man who wrote, "There are many troubles which you can't cure by the Bible and Hymnbook, but which you can cure by a good perspiration and a breath of fresh air." **1888** William S. Burroughs of St. Louis receives a patent for an adding machine. **1944** The Dumbarton Oaks Conference, where the framework for the United Nations will be worked out, opens in Washington, D.C. **1959** Hawaii, consisting of 132 volcanic islands, becomes the nation's fiftieth state.

✦ 22 ✦

1789 President Washington visits the Senate Chamber to ask the senators' "advice and consent" on a treaty, as instructed by the new Constitution. When the senators begin to debate and delay, the president becomes angry and shouts, "This defeats every purpose of my coming here," and thereafter sends written messages, the presidential custom ever since. **1831** Slave preacher Nat Turner leads an uprising in Southampton County, Virginia. Fifty-seven whites are killed, provoking a reprisal and manhunt in which hundreds of blacks are killed. **1851** The yacht *America* wins an international race sponsored by the Royal Yacht Society in England. This will become a traditional international event known as the America's Cup Race.

AUGUST 21

Hawaii celebrates statehood in front of the Iolani Palace, seat of the territorial government. (AP/Wide World Photos)

An exaggerated British view of the burning of Washington. (Library of Congress)

✦ 23 ✦

1630 Wages for construction workers are limited to 2 shillings a day by the Massachusetts Court of Assistants. The law is repealed the next year, and reenacted and extended to farm workers the year after that. **1784** Settlers west of the Alleghenies establish the independent state of Franklin and, under the leadership of John Sevier, attempt to win admission into the Union. By November 1787, Franklin was a lost cause, and the state of North Carolina asserted jurisdiction over the area. In 1796 the area attained a new identity as the state of Tennessee. **1818** The steamboat *Walk-in-the-Water* leaves Buffalo and heads across Lake Erie for Detroit, inaugurating the first steamer service on the Great Lakes.

✦ 24 ✦

1814 A raiding party of British advances on the city of Washington, forcing President Madison and his wife to evacuate. Hours before the British arrive and set fire to the White House, Dolley Madison rescues Gilbert Stuart's portrait of George Washington and the Declaration of Independence. **1857** The failure of an insurance company triggers a financial panic, especially among investors who had been speculating heavily in railroads and real estate. Over the next eighteen months banks close, businesses fail, and the unemployed are seen resorting to barter. **1887** The United States establishes a scientific observation post in Greenland. **1913** Congress authorizes the parcel post system, which will change the way people shop and give an enormous boost to mail order enterprises like Montgomery Ward and Sears, Roebuck.

Colonel Drake, in top hat, at his we in Titusville. (Drake Well Museum)

✦ 25 ✦

1829 The government of Mexico rejects President Andrew Jackson's bid to buy the Mexican state of Texas, which President John Quincy Adams had also tried to purchase. **1928**

AUGUST 24

The Sears, Roebuck catalog, more colorful than the older and staider Montgomery Ward, took rural America by storm. (Sears, Roebuck and Co.)

Naval officer Richard E. Byrd sets off on an exploratory flight to Antarctica. Advancing in cautious stages, Byrd will reach the South Pole from a base camp he names Little America. **1932** Three months after her solo transatlantic flight, Amelia Earhart completes a nineteen-hour, nonstop, transcontinental flight. Her Vega aircraft, designed by John H. Northrup, is the first plane built by the Lockheed Company.

✦ 26 ✦

1859 An unemployed railroad conductor, "Colonel" Edwin L. Drake, strikes oil in Titusville, Pennsylvania, using the first modern oil well, which he built out of a steam engine. Until recently petroleum has been used primarily as a medicinal oil. **1884** A patent is awarded to German immigrant Ottmar Mergenthaler for the invention of the Linotype machine that stamps and casts metal type, replacing manual typesetting and revolutionizing the production of mass circulation newspapers. **1920** The Nineteenth Amendment to the Constitution is ratified: "The right of the citizens of the United States to vote shall not be denied or abridged by the United States or by any state on account of sex." The amendment has been proposed to Congress every year but one since 1868.

✦ 27 ✦

1665 In the first theatrical performance of record in the colonies, *Ye Bear and Ye Cubb* by Alexander Bruce is given at Accomac, Virginia. Three residents are fined for performing in the play. **1776** General Howe's forces outflank the poorly disposed troops of General Washington in the Battle of Long Island and easily beat the Americans. After heavy losses Washington evacuates to Manhattan Island. **1908** Lyndon Baines Johnson, thirty-sixth President and the first Southerner since Woodrow Wilson to hold the office, is born in Johnson City, Texas. **1927** Nicola Sacco and Bartolomeo Vanzetti, politically radical Italian immigrants convicted of killing two men in the robbery of a shoe factory, are executed in Massachusetts after one of the most explosive and controversial trials of the decade.

✦ 28 ✦

1867 The Midway Islands, about 1,200 miles west of Hawaii, are claimed for the United States by Captain William Reynolds of the USS *Lackawanna.* **1963** Over 200,000 people gather in Washington, D.C., to rally for passage of a tough civil rights law. The day's high point comes late in the afternoon when one of the speakers, Dr. Martin Luther King, Jr., departs from his text and elaborates on the theme, "I have a dream": "I have a dream that one day this nation will rise up and live out the true meaning of its creed. . . . I have a dream that one day on the red hills of Georgia the sons of former slaves and the sons of formers slaveowners will be able to sit down together at the table of brotherhood."

✦ 29 ✦

1854 Mechanic Daniel Halladay patents a self-governing windmill that turns to face the wind and controls the speed of its blades, increasing the efficiency of windmills for pumping water and opening new land to farming. **1862** Union Major General John Pope, recently entrusted with command of the Army of Virginia after triumphs further west, clashes with General Stonewall Jackson in the Second Battle of Bull Run. The Union troops suffer twice as many casualties as the Confederates, and Pope is soon relieved of his command. **1893** Whitcomb L. Judson receives a patent for a clasp lock for shoes which, with a little further tinkering, Judson develops into the zipper. **1914** As a protest against the outbreak of war in Europe, 1,500 women dressed in black march to the beat of muffled drums down Fifth Avenue in New York City, displaying a white flag with a dove holding an olive branch.

✦ 30 ✦

1784 The *Empress of China,* under Captain John Greene, arrives in Canton with a load of ginseng in search of a market in China to replace the West Indies, which Britain had closed to American traders. When the *Empress* returns in 1785 with an impres-

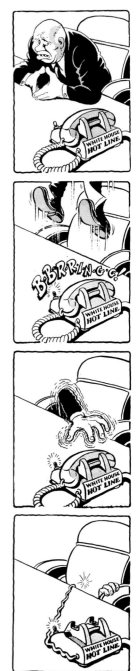

OM HE ... MPLE
.RTS OF THE PEOPLE
DRY SAVED THE UNION
OF ABRAHAM LINCOLN
NSHRINED FOREVER

AUGUST 28

.fter the march on Washington: left
) right, Roy Wilkins of the NAACP,
1artin Luther King, Jr., and veteran
ivil rights leader A. Philip Randolph.
(ohnson Publishing Company)

sive cargo of tea and silks, merchants from Boston to Philadelphia begin making plans for their own expeditions to China. **1963** A hot line telephone link between Washington and Moscow goes into operation, providing direct emergency communication between heads of state as an alternative to diplomatic channels.

✦ 31 ✦

1837 Ralph Waldo Emerson delivers his American Scholar address in Cambridge, Massachusetts, proclaiming that "our day of dependence, our long apprenticeship to the learning of other lands draws to a close." Oliver Wendell Holmes, Sr., later called the speech "our intellectual Declaration of Independence." **1881** The first men's singles tennis championship is held in Newport, Rhode Island. The victor is Richard D. Sears. **1919** Two years after the Bolsheviks seized power in Russia, an American branch of the Communist Party is founded in Chicago.

AUGUST 30

he hot line, as seen by cartoonist
ugh Haynie. (*Courier-Journal* and
uisville Times)

September

✦ 1 ✦

1807 Put on trial for his role in a plot to establish a new country in the southwest, Aaron Burr is acquitted of conspiracy to commit treason. Later, when Americans created the Texas Republic in the same region, Burr remarked, "I was right! I was only thirty years too soon. What was treason in me thirty years ago is patriotism now!" **1859** George Pullman's first sleeping car, a remodeled coach with ten beds, two washrooms, plush upholstery, candle lighting, and heat stoves, makes its first run, between Bloomington, Illinois, and Chicago. Though the response is cool, Pullman continues adding refinements, eventually convincing the public that it is possible to enjoy luxury during long distance travel. **1869** At a convention of nondrinkers in Chicago the Prohibition Party is born. **1916** Congress passes the Keating-Owen Act, which bans from interstate commerce products made with child labor.

SEPTEMBER 1

Pullman brought his sleeping car through several editions, each time increasing the degree of luxury. (New York Public Library)

✦ 2 ✦

1789 The Treasury is the third executive department created by the new government under the new Constitution, following Foreign Affairs (renamed State) under Thomas Jefferson, on July 27, and War, under Henry Knox, on August 7. Alexander Hamilton, President Washington's ally on economic policy, is appointed to head Treasury on September 11. **1795** A group of Connecticut land speculators buys a tract of land in the Western Reserve on the shores of Lake Erie. The following year their agent, Moses Cleaveland, lays out a settlement and names it after himself. (The spelling changes to Cleveland around 1830.) **1945** Japan surrenders formally at ceremonies held aboard the battleship *Missouri,* to end World War II.

✦ 3 ✦

1783 The United States of America signs a peace treaty in Paris with its former motherland. Britain acknowledges the new country's right to all land east of the Mississippi, south of Canada, and north of Florida. **1833** The *New York Sun,* first of the mass-circulation daily newspapers, makes its debut with a novel emphasis on human interest stories. News is "anything that will make people talk," says its editor, Charles A. Dana. **1918** In what are called "slacker raids," uniformed soldiers and sailors in New York and New Jersey stop draft age men at bayonet point and demand to see their draft papers. The raids continue for three days and net over 13,000 "slackers" in New Jersey alone.

✦ 4 ✦

1781 The city of Los Angeles is founded by forty-four settlers from Mexico—eleven men, eleven women, and twenty-two children—on the site of a former Indian village. A pueblo is built and areas for farming and pasture are carefully laid out. **1872** The *New York Sun* breaks the story of the Credit Mobilier scandal, in which Vice President Schuyler Colfax, future president James A. Garfield, and other members of Congress are accused of accepting stock in the Credit Mobilier construction company in return for political favors. **1884** Alfred Thayer Mahan accepts a teaching post at the Naval War College, where he remains little noticed until Theodore Roosevelt embraces his naval theories, and Mahan becomes "the evangelist of sea power." **1888** George Eastman of Rochester, New York, receives a patent for the Kodak camera, which can be held in the hand and uses a continuous roll of film instead of cumbersome individual plates.

✦ 5 ✦

1774 The fifty-six delegates of the First Continental Congress, from every colony except Georgia, gather in a Philadelphia meetinghouse belonging to the city's carpenters to discuss deteriorating relations with the mother country. **1795** In a treaty with the Dey of Algiers, the United States agrees to pay tribute to the Barbary pirates, beginning with a $7 million payment to ransom 115 American sailors. **1882** New York City's Union Square is the site of the nation's first Labor Day parade. A newspaper report addresses the anxiety about a march by 10,000 working people: "Their orderly appearance and sobriety of manner won hearty applause from the spectators who lined the sidewalks."

✦ 6 ✦

1821 Major Jacob Fowler leads a party of twenty men and "thirty Horses and mules Seventeen of Which carried traps and goods for the Indean traid" out of Fort Smith, Arkansas, their destination Santa Fe, to see whether American traders will be tolerated now that Mexico has won its independence from Spain. (The explorer Zebulon Pike had been imprisoned when he crossed into Spanish territory.) In January the men will be officially welcomed and invited to trap beaver, encouraging other traders. **1853** The World's Temperance Convention and Women's Rights Convention, meeting in New York on the same day, come into conflict when the prohibitionists reject an address by Lucy Stone, a leader of the women's group. The prohibitionists also refuse to seat a black minister. **1901** President William McKinley is fatally shot while attending the Pan American Exposition in Buffalo by Leon Czolgosz, a deranged anarchist. **1954** Groundbreaking is held in Shippingport, Pennsylvania, for the world's first nuclear power plant.

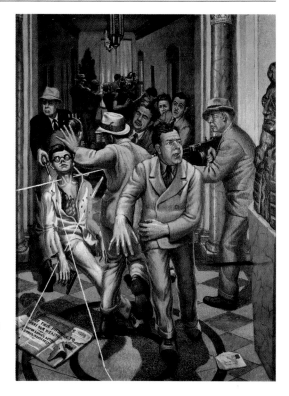

SEPTEMBER 8

Huey Long, foreground, staggers from his wounds, as his bodyguards fire upon Dr. Weiss, the assailant. (John McCrady, Collection of Mr. and Mrs. Keith C. Marshall)

✦ 7 ✦

1888 Jesse James stages his last holdup, striking a westbound Chicago & Alton train at Blue Cut, Missouri. **1892** James J. Corbett knocks out John L. Sullivan in the first professional heavyweight championship fight in which the boxers wear gloves and are required to follow the Marquis of Queensberry rules. The winner's purse is $35,000. **1909** Viennese psychoanalyst Sigmund Freud begins a series of lectures at Clark University in Massachusetts. Later in the week he and his Swiss colleague, Carl Jung, will receive honorary degrees and travel to Niagara Falls.

✦ 8 ✦

1565 The first permanent European settlement in North America is founded at St. Augustine, Florida, under Pedro Menéndez de Avilés, who names it for the saint on whose feast day he first sighted land. Menéndez has also been commanded to drive French Huguenots out of the region, which he soon does. **1935** Louisiana's flamboyant populist governor, Huey Long, embarked on a campaign for the presidency, is assassinated in the state capitol in Baton Rouge by Dr. Carl Weiss, Jr., who feared that Long would become a national dictator.

SEPTEMBER 11
Strollers relax in the Central Park
Mall in the 1890s. (New-York Histor-
ical Society)

✦ 9 ✦

1739 A South Carolina slave named Jemmy tries to lead a band of slaves to freedom in Spanish Florida. The rebels "called out liberty," according to a report of the time, "marched on with Colours displayed, and two drums beating," but were defeated after twenty-five whites were killed. **1776** The Continental Congress replaces the designation "United Colonies" with "United States." **1850** California is admitted to the Union as the thirty-first state. **1919** To protest the suspension of nineteen patrolmen who joined a union, the Boston Police force declares a strike, and 1,117 out of 1,544 officers walk off their jobs. His firm stand against the strike wins national attention for Governor Calvin Coolidge.

✦ 10 ✦

1623 A boatload of lumber and furs, the first cargo from the Plymouth colony, is shipped back to England aboard the *Anne*. **1753** Mohawk Chief Thoyanoguen, known as King Hendrick, addresses a plea to Sir William Johnson, the British superintendent of Indian Affairs: "We don't know what you Christians, English and French intend. We are so hemmed in by you both that we have hardly a hunting place left. In a little while, if we find a bear in a tree, there will immediately appear an owner of the land to claim the property and hinder us from killing it, by which we live. We are so perplexed between you that we hardly know what to say or think."

✦ 11 ✦

1850 The Swedish soprano Jenny Lind makes her American debut at Castle Garden in New York City after an unprece-

nny Lind, the Swedish Nightingale
ho caused a sensation in America,
ortrayed on the cover of sheet
usic. (Theatre Collection, Harvard
ollege Library)

ing Hendrick. (Library of Congress)

dentedly lavish promotional campaign by her American manager, P. T. Barnum. Barnum auctions off tickets to the event, the first ticket going for $225. **1857** Frederick Law Olmsted, who has failed in careers in writing, publishing, and farming, is appointed superintendent of New York's Central Park, a position which releases his genius as a pioneer landscape architect. **1897** Twenty are killed in shooting between deputy sheriffs and striking coal miners in Hazleton and Latimer, Pennsylvania. The strike ends in one of the first victories for the United Mine Workers and establishes an eight-hour work day, bimonthly salary checks, and an end to company stores.

✦ 12 ✦

1798 Newspaper editor Benjamin (Lightning Rod Junior) Bache, grandson of Benjamin Franklin, is charged with violating the Sedition Act for his writing about President John Adams. When Thomas Jefferson becomes president, he will issue a general pardon to everyone convicted under the act. **1860** William Walker, one of the American adventurers known as filibusters for their interference in the affairs of other countries, meets his end in Honduras, where he is executed by firing squad for his attempt to overthrow the government. **1944** The U.S. Army crosses the border at Aachen, entering Germany for the first time in World War II.

✦ 13 ✦

1609 Henry Hudson, exploring the harbor at New York on his way back from a search for a Northwest Passage, ventures up the river that will eventually receive his name, reaching the site of Albany on September 19. Indians, most of them friendly, paddle out on canoes to offer gifts and items for trade. **1826** William Murray, a bricklayer who threatened to expose the secrets of the Masonic Order, disappears in upstate New York. The uproar that follows reveals widespread anxiety about the Masons, and leads to the formation of an Anti-Masonic political party. **1845** The Knickerbocker Baseball Club is founded in New York, the first to play by formal rules, which include underhand pitching, an out on balls caught on the first bounce, and victory to the first team to score twenty-one aces (runs).

✦ 14 ✦

1781 Frances Count de Grasse, commanding the French West Indian fleet, leads his ships up Chesapeake Bay to meet Washington's army and transport it to Williamsburg. From there the combined army of about 9,000 Americans and 7,800 French troops will begin the siege of Yorktown. **1814** Francis Scott Key of Baltimore, who was detained on a British ship during the unsuccessful bombardment of Fort McHenry, is inspired by his experience to write *The Star Spangled Banner.* He sets the words to a British tune called *Anacreon in Heaven.* **1957** President Eisenhower intervenes in the Little Rock, Arkansas, school crisis, where Governor Orval Faubus has called out the National Guard to prevent black students from entering Central High School.

SEPTEMBER 16
The starting line of the Cherokee Strip land rush was photographed seconds after the signal was given. (Archives and Manuscripts Division of the Oklahoma Historical Society)

✦ 15 ✦

1776 As General Washington evacuates his troops to northern Manhattan, the British arrive at Kips' Bay, nearly cutting off the American Army. New York again becomes a British city and will remain so until November 1783. **1853** The Congregational Church of South Butler, New York, ordains Antoinette Brown, America's first female minister. One of the early graduates of Oberlin College, the nation's first coeducational college, Brown is the future sister-in-law of Elizabeth Blackwell, the first American woman to graduate from a medical college. **1857** William Howard Taft, America's twenty-seventh president, is born in Cincinnati. His greatest happiness will be a seat on the Supreme Court after his retirement from politics: "Presidents come and go, but the Court goes on forever." **1959** Soviet Premier Nikita Khrushchev begins a tumultuous six-day visit that includes tours of cities and farms.

✦ 16 ✦

1620 The *Mayflower* departs Plymouth, England, aiming for Virginia, with 101 passengers aboard, most of them not Puritans, including Miles Standish, hired as military leader, and several indentured servants and craftsmen. **1853** The immigrant German piano maker Henry Engelhard Steinway (then spelled Steinweg) sells his first American-made piano. In the next few years Steinway and his sons perfect the iron-frame piano, leading to an instrument with a full and brilliant sound. **1893** The Cherokee Strip, a section of the Oklahoma Territory, is the site of a land rush that entitles settlers to claim 160-acre parcels simply by planting a flag. By day's end 40,000 sites have been claimed on what was, until then, Indian territory off-limits to white settlement. **1898** In Indianapolis lawyer Albert Beveridge advocates conquest of the Philippines in a speech called The March of the Flag, regarded as the classic expression of American imperialism. **1940** Selective Service goes into effect, requiring males between 21 and 35 to register for the draft.

SEPTEMBER 14

In 1914, Fort McHenry's battered flag was repaired for exhibition at the Smithsonian Institution. Here the flag is being sewed to a linen backing. (Smithsonian Institution)

✦ 17 ✦

1787 The Constitution is signed by all but three delegates to the Convention. "The business being closed," George Washington wrote in his diary, "the members adjourned to the City Tavern, dined together and took a cordial leave of each other; after which I returned to my lodgings . . . and retired to meditate on the momentous work which had been executed. . . ." **1862** The Battle of Antietam: McClellan meets Lee at Sharpsburg, Maryland, and puts a stop to the Confederate Army's northward advance but fumbles an opportunity to defeat Lee altogether. In a single day there are 23,000 casualties, in terms of human loss America's costliest day. **1978** An accord between Egypt and Israel is signed at Camp David, Maryland, after negotiations overseen by President Jimmy Carter.

SEPTEMBER 17

In this painting of Antietam by Union soldier James Hope, Confederate batteries fire on Sumner's troops who are advancing toward Dunker Church, left. (Edward Owen/National Park Service)

✦ 18 ✦

1759 French Quebec surrenders to the British after a calamitous battle on the Plains of Abraham, extinguishing French hopes of dominating North America. **1850** The "compromise" Fugitive Slave Act becomes law, providing that special federal commissioners can demand the assistance of bystanders in capturing runaway slaves, and that citizens who assist fugitives are subject to a $1,000 fine, six-month jail term, and damages of $1,000 per fugitive. **1850** The first edition of the *New York Daily Times* goes on sale. The paper drops "Daily" from its name in 1857. **1889** Social reformer Jane Addams moves into Hull House in Chicago, America's first settlement house. "Probably no young matron ever placed her own things in her own house with more pleasure than that with which we first furnished Hull House," she wrote.

✦ 19 ✦

1752 Three hundred German immigrants arrive in Massachusetts, reports the *Boston Evening Post*, including "a number of men skilled in the making of Glass, of various sorts." **1796** A Philadelphia newspaper, the *Daily American Advertiser*, devotes its second page to President Washington's Farewell Address, which was never actually delivered as a speech. **1844** Government surveyors working near Lake Superior discover the Mesabi iron range when they notice a compass deviating 87 degrees from normal. **1926** A hurricane sweeps Florida, causing 372 deaths and destroying thousands of houses. It temporarily disrupts the state's land boom, in which thousands of acres, aggressively promoted but often undeveloped and uninspected by the buyers, were being sold as shares in a tropical paradise.

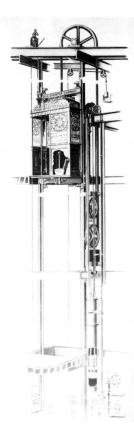

✦ 20 ✦

1839 The steamer *British Queen* brings news of the daguerreotype process of photography, and within days Americans are at work making pictures. **1853** The construction of public buildings is revolutionized when inventor Elisha Otis demonstrates his "safety elevator," which does not fall even when its cable is cut. **1873** In the aftermath of the shocking failure of Jay Cooke & Company, which was involved in financing the Northern Pacific Railroad, the New York Stock Exchange is forced to close for the first time to contain the spreading panic.

TEMBER 20

early model of Otis' passenger
vator. (Archive, United Technolo-
s Corporation)

✦ 21 ✦

1595 The earliest record of European settlement in New Mexico is a petition of this day by Don Juan de Onate to the vice-regal government at Mexico, requesting assistance in establishing a colony on the Rio del Norte with the goal of converting and enslaving the native population. **1846** Manhattan retailer A. T. Stewart opens an immense dry goods store, featuring fixed prices and merchandise organized into departments. Philip Hone was most amazed by the store's plate glass display windows—"a most extraordinary, and I think useless, piece of extravagance." **1893** Bicycle maker Charles E. Duryea and his brother, Frank, demonstrate their prototype for America's first successful gasoline-powered automobile by driving through the streets of Springfield, Massachusetts. **1981** President Ronald Reagan appoints Sandra Day O'Connor of California an associate justice of the Supreme Court, the first woman to serve on the court.

PTEMBER 21

harles Duryea poses aboard his

s-powered automobile. (Brown

'others)

✦ 22 ✦

1776 Connecticut schoolteacher Nathan Hale is hanged by the British after providing General Washington with information on British troop positions. Hale's career as a spy, which he entered with some reluctance, lasted nine days. His famous last words are said to have been inspired by Joseph Addison: "What a pity is it/That we can die but once to save our country!" **1784** Russian trappers establish a colony on Kodiak Island, Alaska. **1785** The first survey of national lands begins along the Ohio River in the Territory of Ohio. Townships are laid out in a grid pattern of six square miles, with lots to be offered for $1 an acre. One section in each township had to be set aside for a public school.

✦ 23 ✦

1779 Captain John Paul Jones, operating as a privateer aboard an old French ship he has renamed *Bonhomme Richard* in honor of Ben Franklin, sights a convoy of thirty-nine merchant ships off the coast of England. He begins firing at the lead ship, but his own ship takes the worst of it. When asked to surrender, he replies, "Sir, I have not yet begun to fight," and continues firing through the *Richard*'s flames until H.M.S. *Serapis* surrenders. **1938** A time capsule is buried on the site of the New York World's Fair, to be opened in the year 6939 to reveal such artifacts as a Bible, a mail-order catalog, and newsreels of President Franklin Roosevelt and a college football game. **1952** With his political career in jeopardy because of a secret campaign slush fund, Vice President Richard M. Nixon addresses the nation on television, insisting he never benefited personally from the fund and is guilty only of accepting a pet dog, Checkers, which he will not give back.

✦ 24 ✦

1869 A plot by Jay Gould and James Fisk to corner the gold market reaches its denouement in Black Friday, when the scheme backfires and the market price of bullion plummets. Gould and Fisk thought they had persuaded President Grant to halt the sale of government bullion, but when Grant changed his mind and ordered a sale, gold hoarders saw their investments shrink almost overnight. **1956** The first transatlantic telephone cable is completed. **1963** The U.S. Senate gives its consent to the nuclear test ban treaty signed by the United States, Soviet Union, and Britain but not France.

SEPTEMBER 22

Nathan Hale drummed to the gallows by British troops. (Morristown National Historical Park)

✦ 25 ✦

1493 Christopher Columbus sails from Cadiz on a second voyage to the New World, grander than the first, with seventeen ships, six priests to convert the natives, and hundreds of laymen hoping to establish a colony. **1513** Vasco Núñez de Balboa crosses the Isthmus of Panama from a Spanish trading post in the Caribbean and discovers the Pacific Ocean, which he claims for Spain. **1690** *Publick Occurrences Both Foreign and Domestick,* the first newspaper in the colonies, appears in Boston—but it is closed down four days later, on the grounds that the publisher lacked government permission for his venture. **1890** Spurred by the writings of John Muir and U.S. Geologic Survey director John Wesley Powell, who argued that the federal government was responsible for protecting the environment, Congress creates Yosemite National Park in California.

SEPTEMBER 25

Herrera's *Historia General* depicts Balboa's passage across Panama to the Pacific. (Rare Book Division, New York Public Library)

✦ 26 ✦

1772 The New Jersey colony makes it illegal to practice medicine without a license. **1789** John Jay, a proponent of the new Constitution and author of Number 5 of the Federalist Papers, is confirmed as the first chief justice of the Supreme Court. **1914** The Federal Trade Commission, intended to regulate interstate business aggressively and especially to crack down on fraud and price fixing, replaces the more low-key Bureau of Corporations. **1918** Every available American troop unit is

SEPTEMBER 26

American supply convoys gather for the massive operation at Esnes, near the Meuse. (National Archives)

used to drive the Germans into retreat in the area between the
Meuse River and Argonne Forest. The operation, involving
over 1 million men, lasts until the armistice goes into effect on
November 11.

✦ 27 ✦

1817 After decades of resistance to the influx of white settlers,
the Ohio Indians submit to a treaty that requires the surrender
of 4 million acres. **1854** The passenger ship *Arctic* collides with
a French steamship off Newfoundland, and nearly all 200 passengers drown while crew members monopolize the lifeboats.
Indignation over the *Arctic* disaster leads to demands that passenger ships be built with watertight compartments. **1912** The
first published blues music, W. C. Handy's "Memphis Blues,"
goes on sale in Memphis, Tennessee. **1964** The Warren Commission releases a 296,000-word report on its investigation into
the assassination of President John F. Kennedy, concluding that
Lee Harvey Oswald "acted alone" in killing the president.

✦ 28 ✦

1542 The Portuguese explorer João Rodrigues Cabrillo sails into San Diego harbor and lands near Ballast Point, which qualifies him as the European discoverer of California. **1774** Joseph Galloway of Pennsylvania proposes a plan by which America would be granted something like dominion status since, he argues, "the colonies hold in abhorrence the idea of being considered independent communities." The proposal is defeated in the Continental Congress by a single vote and is later expunged from the congressional minutes. **1829** Free black David Walker publishes *Walker's Appeal,* a radical antislavery essay that calls for worldwide uprising by slaves against their masters: "It is no more harm for you to kill a man, who is trying to kill you, than it is for you to take a drink of water when you are thirsty." **1850** Congress abolishes flogging in the U.S. Navy and on merchant vessels.

✦ 29 ✦

1690 William Bradford, a Philadelphia printer, and William Rittenhouse, a German immigrant papermaker, lease a twenty-acre site for construction of America's first paper mill. **1789** Congress establishes the United States Army, 700 strong, in response to Article I, Section 8 of the new Constitution, which gives it the power "To raise and support Armies." **1925** In Washington testimony Army Colonel William "Billy" Mitchell proposes the creation of an independent military branch for aviation and describes the present military command as incompetent. Mitchell is court-martialed over his remarks, found guilty of conduct prejudicial to military discipline, and suspended for five years. In 1942 he is posthumously rehabilitated and promoted to the rank of major general.

✦ 30 ✦

1630 John Billington, hanged after being convicted of shooting a man to death in a quarrel, is the first criminal to be executed in the English colonies. **1787** Captain Robert Gray departs Boston aboard the *Columbia* on the first circumnavigation of the globe by an American ship. **1846** Dr. William Morton, a dentist, uses ether as an anesthetic for the first time. **1855** Mormon leader Brigham Young commands that pilgrims to Utah must give up their expensive horse and oxen-drawn wagons and push handcarts along the route. For some who got a late start, the slow progress of the handcarts leads to death from winter storms and Indian attacks.

SEPTEMBER 30

A few weeks after Dr. William Morton's successful testing of ether as an anesthetic, there was a public demonstration at Massachusetts General Hospital. In this painting by Robert Hinckley, Morton is seen holding a bottle of ether while the prominent surgeon John Warren makes an incision. (Boston Medical Library in the Francis A. Countway Library of Medicine)

✦ 1 ✦

1810 The Berkshire Cattle Show, one of the nation's first county agricultural fairs, opens in Pittsfield, Massachusetts. **1847** Twenty-eight-year-old Maria Mitchell, a Nantucket librarian and amateur astronomer, discovers a comet which is later named after her. **1880** John Philip Sousa becomes conductor of the U.S. Marine Corps Band. **1896** After a hard-fought campaign by organized farmers, who were supported by Postmaster General John Wanamaker, the department store magnate, the post office begins rural free delivery, making it possible for people outside cities to receive mail at home (and resulting in the closing of many small post offices). **1924** James Earl Carter, Jr., thirty-ninth president of the United States, is born in Plains, Georgia, son of a farmer/grocer and a nurse.

✦ 2 ✦

1535 Explorer Jacques Cartier lands at the site of Montreal, then called Hochelaga, on his second voyage in search of gold and "other riches." **1780** Major John André of the British Army is hanged as a spy. André, who controlled a small network of informants in the colonies, was currently involved in a plot with the disgruntled American general Benedict Arnold. **1889** Delegates of all Western Hemisphere nations except Canada and the Dominican Republic meet at the first Pan American Conference in Washington.

OCTOBER 9 *(Opening illustration)*
1820 engraving of the Siege of Yorktown. (Anne S. K. Brown Military
Collection, Brown University Library)

OCTOBER 1
A mail wagon along one of the rural
routes opened by Rural Free Delivery. (Brown Brothers)

OCTOBER 1
Maria Mitchell, the first woman
elected to the American Academy of
Arts and Sciences, with an assistant
at the Vassar College Observatory,
where she became professor of as-
tronomy. (Vassar College Library)

✦ **3** ✦

1650 Faced by aggressive competition from Dutch merchants,
Parliament acts to require non-British merchants to obtain a
permit for trading in the colonies. **1684** After customs collector Edward Randolph reports that the colonists are ignoring
the Navigation Acts and abusing the Church of England, King
Charles II begins proceedings to revoke the charter of the Massachusetts Bay Colony. This will lead to the appointment of the
hated Sir Edmund Andros as governor of all the New England
colonies. **1922** Mrs. W. H. Felton of Georgia is appointed U.S.
senator to serve out the term of a deceased incumbent. The
appointment makes her the nation's first female member of the
Senate, although her term lasts only one day.

✦ **4** ✦

1733 An advertisement in the *New York Gazette and Mercury*
offers "the highest price" for linen rags, which are sought by a
paper mill desperate for raw material. Not until the nineteenth
century was the manufacture of paper from wood pulp per-
fected. **1822** Rutherford B. Hayes, the nineteenth President of
the United States, is born in Delaware, Ohio. Victor in the
disputed election of 1876, whose outcome was not determined
until the following March, Hayes was known in some quarters
as His Fraudulency. **1965** Pope Paul VI arrives in the United
States to deliver an appeal for world peace at the UN General
Assembly. His schedule includes a visit to the world's fair and
officiating at a service in Yankee Stadium.

✦ 5 ✦

1830 Chester A. Arthur, twenty-first president of the United States, is born in Fairfield, Vermont. Arthur built his power by controlling patronage in New York, but once in the White House he broke with machine politics and introduced civil service reform. Said one former ally, "He isn't 'Chet' Arthur any more, he's the president." **1877** Chief Joseph of the Nez Perce and about 400 followers surrender to the U.S. Cavalry near the Bear Paw Mountains, forty miles from the Canadian border, after a three-month chase. "Hear me, my chiefs," said Joseph. "I am tired. My heart is sick and sad. From where the sun now stands, I will fight no more forever." **1953** Earl Warren, Republican governor of California, is sworn in as chief justice of the Supreme Court.

✦ 6 ✦

1683 Thirteen Mennonite families from the Rhineland, the first German immigrants to America, arrive in Pennsylvania, founding a community near Philadelphia called Germantown. **1866** The nation's first train robbery gang, the four Reno brothers (a fifth brother was never involved), commit their first recorded stickup when they open two safes and take $13,000 from a moving Ohio & Mississippi Railway train. **1927** The first widely seen talking movie, *The Jazz Singer*, loosely based on the life of its star, Al Jolson, has its premiere in New York.

✦ 7 ✦

1763 By a proclamation of King George III, England reserves the land between the Alleghenies and the Mississippi River for Indians, thus closing the West to colonial settlement. **1783** Virginia's House of Burgesses grants freedom to slaves who fought in the Continental Army during the American Revolution. **1826** In a project that launches the American granite industry, the first American railroad begins operation: Horse-drawn wagons haul granite blocks three miles along a metal-plated wooden track from a quarry in Quincy, Massachusetts, to the Neponset River, where barges carry the blocks to the construction site of the Bunker Hill Monument in Charlestown.

✦ 8 ✦

1871 A fire breaks out in a barn belonging to Patrick O'Leary of Chicago and spreads quickly through the drought-stricken city, most of whose buildings are made of wood. High winds carry the flames during the night, and the next day before rain begins to fall, the blaze has reached the prairie north of the city. Nearly one third of the city's 300,000 residents are left homeless and 300 people are killed. Spared is the Water Tower (today a much-loved landmark), and Chicago rebuilds rapidly. **1942** The first group of WAVES (Women Appointed for Voluntary Emergency Service) reports for training at Smith College.

✦ 9 ✦

1779 Count Casimir Pulaski, the exiled Polish patriot who became commander of an independent cavalry unit in Washington's army, is killed during an attempt to retake Savannah from the British. **1781** American and French troops begin firing on General Cornwallis' fortifications at Yorktown, Virginia. **1865** The nation's first working underground oil pipeline is completed between Oil Creek and Pithole, Pennsylvania. **1917** Clarence Saunders of Memphis, owner of a grocery called Piggly Wiggly, is granted a patent for his self-service method of operation, which anticipates the supermarket.

✦ 10 ✦

1845 The Naval School opens at Fort Severn, Annapolis, Maryland, as an alternative to the training of naval officers through an often-brutal apprenticeship at sea. In 1850 the school's name is changed to the U.S. Naval Academy. **1913** In a ceremony at the White House President Wilson pushes a button that sets off an explosion at a dike in Panama. With that blast, the waterway across the isthmus of Panama is completed. The canal will open to traffic the following year. **1918** Members of Western tribes, including Cheyenne, Oto, Comanche, Kiowa, and Apache Indians, form the First American Church in El Reno, Oklahoma. **1973** Vice President Spiro Agnew resigns from office after pleading no contest to a charge of tax evasion.

✦ 11 ✦

1833 The First U.S. Dragoons, the nation's first cavalry outfit, assembles near St. Louis under the command of Colonel Henry Dodge, with Jefferson Davis as adjutant. **1868** Telegraph operator Thomas Edison receives his first patent, for a telegraphic device that records the votes of legislators electrically. It proves unpopular with politicians, who fear that automatic tabulation would limit their opportunities to filibuster. **1906** The San Francisco Board of Education orders that Oriental children be separated into segregated schools. Under pressure from President Roosevelt the city's mayor later rescinds the order, in return for an agreement by the president to discourage Japanese immigration. **1950** CBS receives government authorization to broadcast programs in color.

✦ 12 ✦

1492 Christopher Columbus touches land on Guanahani or Samana Cay in the Bahamas and names it San Salvador, claiming it for Spain. Columbus is convinced he has reached the Far East. **1753** The *Maryland Gazette* runs an ad offering the artistic services of A. Pooley: "Either in the Limning Way, History, Altar Pieces for Churches, Landscapes, Views of their own Houses and Estates, Signs or any other Way of Painting, and also Gilding." **1792** The nation's first memorial to Columbus is dedicated in Baltimore.

OCTOBER 10
Building the Panama Canal, which was talked of as early as the California Gold Rush, began in 1906, and formally opened in 1914. (Bettmann Archive)

✦ 13 ✦

1761 Colonel Henry Bouquet of the western frontier outpost of Fort Pitt bans settlement or hunting by whites in any of the territory reserved for Indians by the Treaty of Easton. **1792** The cornerstone is laid for the President's Palace, later renamed the White House. Designed by James Hoban, the building is modeled after the Irish mansion of the Duke of Leinster, with the east and west porticos built from designs by Benjamin Henry Latrobe. **1903** Big Bill Dineen strikes out Honus Wagner, and Boston beats Pittsburgh, 5 to 3, to conclude the first World Series.

OCTOBER 16
Joseph Saxton's daguerreotype, taken in 1839, marks the beginnings of photography in America. (Historical Society of Pennsylvania)

✦ 14 ✦

1774 At the Continental Congress in Philadelphia, in formal session since September 5, delegates disagree on how to proceed in the crisis but join together in a Declaration of Rights that denounces Britain's taxes and punitive laws and sets forth ten statements of colonists' rights, among them "life, liberty and property," which the British government has no right to interfere with. **1842** The opening of Croton Aqueduct, extending thirty miles to the north, brings New York City its first public water supply but doesn't put out of business the merchants who sell spring water by the bucket. Philadelphia has had city water since 1801. **1890** The thirty-third president of the United States, David Dwight Eisenhower, known afterward as Dwight David, is born in Denison, Texas, where his father works as a mechanic in the railroad yards. **1947** Air Force Captain Charles Yeager, flying a Bell X-1, becomes the first person to fly faster than the speed of sound.

✦ 15 ✦

1776 The New York Provincial Convention orders that all tanned hides be evacuated north of the Highlands and carefully guarded, because of a critical lack of shoes and shoe leather. On December 4 the Continental Congress is told that at Fort Ticonderoga there are 900 pairs of shoes for over 12,000 men. **1878** The first electric light company, Edison Electric, is organized in New York City with the backing of financier J. P. Morgan. Edison's plan is to create a centralized system for generating and transmitting electricity that can compete as a power source with natural gas. It is 1882 before his first power plant begins operation. **1965** Nationwide demonstrations against the war in Vietnam begin in California, where 10,000 people march in protest to the Oakland Army base.

OCTOBER 16

captured during the government's attack on Harpers Ferry, John Brown said at his trial, "It is a great comfort to feel assured that I am permitted to die for a cause." (Western Reserve Historical Society, Cleveland)

✦ 16 ✦

1701 Yale College is founded in New Haven, Connecticut, as the Collegiate School by Congregationalists who are unhappy with the doctrinal liberalism of Harvard. **1839** The earliest known surviving American photograph is taken by Joseph Saxton, a mechanic at the United States Mint in Philadelphia, who built his camera out of a cigar box and magnifying glass. **1859** Radical abolitionist John Brown and some eighteen followers attack the federal arsenal at Harpers Ferry, Virginia, hoping to arm themselves for large-scale raids on slave plantations in the state. But slaves do not flock to him, and within two days the rebels are surrounded by federal troops and all but wiped out. **1916** The nation's first birth control clinic is opened in Brooklyn, New York, by Margaret Sanger, Fania Mindell, and Ethel Burne. **1940** Benjamin Oliver Davis, Sr., becomes the first black general in the U.S. Army.

✦ 17 ✦

1777 General John Burgoyne, in retreat since his defeat ten days earlier at Freeman's Farm, surrenders his army at Saratoga, New York. Lost to the British are not only Burgoyne's 5,000 troops; the defeat also spells the end to the British strategy of dividing the colonies along the Hudson. **1787** Prince Hall, community organizer and founder of the first black chapter of the Masons, petitions the Massachusetts legislature for equal school facilities: "We must fear for our rising offspring to see them in ignorance in a land of gospel light." **1845** President James K. Polk appoints a consul in Monterey whose principal responsibility will be to create an atmosphere favorable to annexation of California. **1933** German physicist Albert Einstein arrives in the United States to make his home in Princeton, New Jersey, where the new Institute for Advanced Studies offers a haven for scholars who are fleeing the Nazi regime.

✦ 18 ✦

1648 The shoemakers of Boston form a labor organization, a guildlike combination of master workers trying to maintain a monopoly on their profession. **1776** Polish aristocrat Thaddeus Kosciuszko is appointed colonel of engineers in the Revolutionary Army. His fortifications at West Point will make that key position well-nigh impregnable. **1797** The XYZ affair

OCTOBER 17
Albert Einstein takes the oath of citizenship in Trenton, New Jersey. (AP/Wide World Photos)

eneral Douglas MacArthur (left)
eps off a landing craft to the shore
Leyte Island and proclaims: "Peo-
e of the Philippines, I have re-
rned." (Library of Congress)

brings American relations with France from amity to near-war
when three treaty negotiators are approached by representatives of Foreign Minister Talleyrand and asked for a $240,000
bribe in exchange for a French agreement to stop interfering
with American shipping. The three bribe solicitors are desig-
nated X, Y, and Z in diplomatic dispatches.

✦ 19 ✦

1781 General Charles Cornwallis surrenders at Yorktown, all
but ending Britain's claims to govern the thirteen colonies.
1847 The cornerstone is laid for the Washington Monument, a
publicly funded project whose completion will take thirty-eight
years. George Templeton Strong, who attended the ceremony,
was unimpressed by the planned design: "Some architecture is
'music turned into stone': this might be poetically described as
the creak and whizz and pounding of a big steam engine petri-
fied, so angular and stiff and prosaic it is." **1864** In the north-
ernmost engagement of the Civil War, a band of Confederate
prisoners who had escaped to Canada attacks the town of St.
Albans, Vermont, stealing horses and robbing banks before retreating across the border.

✦ 20 ✦

1818 The United States and Britain sign a treaty that sets the
United States-Canada border at the 49th parallel except for the
land west of the Rockies, which is to be held jointly for ten
years. **1944** General Douglas MacArthur fulfills his promise to
return to the Philippines as U.S. troops attack Leyte Island.
Although a naval battle in support of the invasion will disable a
major part of Japan's sea power within a week, reconquest of
the Philippines takes another eight months. **1947** The House
Un-American Activities Committee opens public hearings into
Communist influence in Hollywood, laying the groundwork for
a blacklist of suspected subversives in the movie industry.

✦ 21 ✦

1872 German Emperor William I arbitrates a territorial dispute between the United States and Canada, awarding the San
Juan Islands in the northwest to the United States. **1944** After
several days of house-to-house fighting, Aachen, the first German city to fall, surrenders to the Allies.

✦ 22 ✦

1844 The Day of Second Coming prophesied by William
Miller comes and goes, but his undiscouraged followers go on
to form the Seventh-Day Adventist Church. **1845** Journalist,
poet, and former teacher Walt Whitman appraises the public
schools in the *Brooklyn Evening Star*: "As a general thing the
faults of our public school system are—crowding too many
students together, insufficiency of books, and their cost being
taxed directly on the pupil—and the flogging system, which in
a portion of the schools still holds its wretched sway." **1883** It
is the first opening night for the Metropolitan Opera House in
New York City, where the program is Gounod's *Faust*. **1938**
Inventor Chester F. Carlson produces the first Xerox image but
has trouble interesting investors in the process.

✦ 23 ✦

1803 John Quincy Adams, currently a member of the Senate in
the new nation's capital, notes that "there is no church of any
denomination in this city; but religious service is usually performed on Sundays at the Treasury office and at the Capitol."
1906 Oscar S. Straus becomes the first Jew to hold a cabinet
appointment when Theodore Roosevelt names him secretary of
commerce and labor. **1945** Jackie Robinson, the first black

baseball player to be hired by a major league team, is signed to a contract by Branch Rickey, general manager of the Brooklyn Dodgers, and assigned to their farm team in Montreal.

✦ **24** ✦

1776 The Hanover Presbytery of Virginia, calling for "the free exercise of religion according to the dictates of our consciences," becomes the first religious body to embrace the Declaration of Independence. **1861** East and West coasts are linked by telegraph at Fort Bridger, Utah, as the first transcontinental telegraph message is sent from San Francisco to President Lincoln in Washington. **1929** Panic selling on Wall Street takes a new leap on Black Thursday, when almost 13 million shares are traded on the New York Stock Exchange. The House of Morgan forms a buying pool to shore up prices, but after a brief rally panic sets in again

OCTOBER 24
The New York Stock Exchange on Black Thursday, a vertiginous view.
(Library of Congress)

✦ 25 ✦

1864 Private John W. Haley of the 17th Maine Regiment writes from the neighborhood of Petersburg, Virginia, where the Union Army has been laying siege to the town since June: "Got up early, expecting to be soon on the road. We packed up, but hour after hour passed and no order came. Thus the day wore away, with us lying in the dust up to our ears. The heat and suspense were almost unbearable. . . . During the day the teams arrived with fresh rations and ammunition. The artillery and teams also came up from City Point and moved toward the left, setting in motion a fresh rumor that we are going to make a heavy attack somewhere on the left. But we have seen enough of Grant to know that what we *expect* of him is just the last thing he will do. . . ." **1946** Facing demands for housing from returning veterans and others who waited during the war, President Harry Truman declares a state of emergency in housing and lifts import restrictions on lumber, but the shortage eases only when builders develop new ways to produce inexpensive tract housing on a large scale.

✦ 26 ✦

1749 In the first explicit legal recognition of slavery in the British colonies, Parliament legalizes slavery in Georgia, where it had been prohibited by the original charter. **1825** Seven years after construction began, the Erie Canal opens a water

OCTOBER 26
The Erie Canal at Lockport, New York, with wooden lock gates and, at left, a hotel for canal travelers. (New York Public Library)

OCTOBER 27
James Madison, father of the Constitution, in a portrait by Charles Willson Peale. (The Thomas Gilcrease Institute of American History and Art, Tulsa)

route from the Hudson River to Lake Erie that links the Midwest to the Atlantic coast. The massive project, which had been financed by the state of New York after it was spurned by the federal government, soon proves its worth by making New York City the nation's commercial center, and its success sets off a boom in canal building.

✦ 27 ✦

1787 The first of seventy-seven essays explaining the new Constitution and urging ratification appears in a New York newspaper. Signed by "Publius," the essays are written by Alexander Hamilton, James Madison, and John Jay and are published collectively the following May as *The Federalist Papers.* **1858** Theodore Roosevelt, twenty-seventh president of the United States, is born in New York City. **1904** The city of New York opens the world's first underground and underwater subway system. **1916** The entertainment industry journal *Variety* notes a new musical form: "Chicago has added another innovation to its list of discoveries in the so-called 'jazz band.'" Although jazz has flourished for some years in New Orleans, this is the first appearance of the term in print.

✦ 28 ✦

1636 Harvard College is founded in Cambridge, Massachusetts: "When any scholar is able to understand Tully or such like classical author extempore, and make and speak true Latin in verse and prose . . . and decline perfectly the paradigms of nouns and verbs in the Greek tongue, let him then and not before, be capable of admission into the college." For several generations the school's primary purpose is to train ministers. **1646** The missionary Reverend John Eliot conducts the first Protestant service for Indians in Nonantum, Massachusetts. Eliot will work thirty years on a translation of the Bible into the Algonquian language. **1886** The Statue of Liberty, called *Liberty Enlightening the World,* by sculptor Frédéric Auguste Bartholdi, is dedicated in ceremonies at Bedloe's Island in New York Harbor.

OCTOBER 28
Excursion boats crowd together in the fog to provide views of Liberty on its dedication day. (National Park Service, Statue of Liberty National Monument)

✦ 29 ✦

1796 Captain Ebenezer Dorr of Boston sails the *Otter* into Monterey Bay. It is the first U.S. ship to enter a California port. **1872** J. S. Risdon of Genoa, Illinois, patents an all-metal windmill, but the new invention makes slow headway against its traditional wooden competitor. **1923** *Runnin' Wild,* a musical that introduced the Charleston, opens on Broadway. **1929** After a week of panic selling and halfhearted rallies, the bottom falls out of the stock market, and over 16 million shares are unloaded. **1947** The General Electric Company uses dry ice to seed clouds and produce rain in Concord, New Hampshire.

✦ 30 ✦

1735 John Adams, second president of the United States, is born in Braintree, Massachusetts. Ever outspoken, Adams was called by Benjamin Franklin "always an honest man, often a wise one, but sometimes, and in some things, absolutely out of his senses." **1840** Ralph Waldo Emerson writes to British essayist Thomas Carlyle about the social experiments becoming fashionable in American literary circles: "Not a reading man but has a draft of a new community in his waistcoat pocket. . . . One man renounces the use of animal food; and another of coin; and another of domestic hired service, and another of the State." **1938** Actor and director Orson Welles broadcasts a dramatization of H. G. Wells' *War of the Worlds* on the radio. Widely mistaken for news of an actual invasion from outer space, it leads to widespread panic.

✦ 31 ✦

1684 A royal customs collector is murdered by George Talbot, a nephew of the proprietor of the Maryland colony, Lord Baltimore. Baltimore is fined £2,500 for the offense, and his nephew is sent into exile from the colony for five years. Despite his pecadillos, a Maryland county is named for Talbot. **1864** Nevada is admitted to the Union as the thirty-sixth state, its admission a special priority of the Lincoln administration, which is counting votes that will be needed to ratify a constitutional amendment banning slavery.

✦ 1 ✦

1848 The Boston Female Medical School opens with twelve students and continues as such until a merger with Boston University in 1874. **1861** The aged General Winfield Scott, hero of the war with Mexico, is replaced as commander in chief of the Federal Armies by George McClellan. Scott laid the strategy that the Union Army will follow throughout the war: a major army in northern Virginia to protect the capital and hold back the Confederates; a naval blockade; and a Mississippi River operation to divide the Confederacy—the so-called Anaconda policy, to defeat the South by strangulation.

✦ 2 ✦

1795 James K. Polk, eleventh president of the United States, is born in Pineville, North Carolina. **1865** Warren G. Harding, twenty-ninth president of the United States, is born in Blooming Grove, Morrow County, Ohio. "I am a man of limited talents from a small town," he once said of himself. **1889** After almost two decades of arguing over the location of a capital city and other disputes that signaled irreconcilable differences, North and South Dakota are admitted to the Union as separate states, the thirty-ninth (North Dakota) and fortieth to join. **1920** KDKA in Pittsburgh begins the nation's first radio

NOVEMBER 14 *(Opening illustration)*
Thomas Edison's pioneer research laboratory at Menlo Park, New Jersey. Edison is seated at center, wearing a cap. (Detail, Henry Ford Museum and Greenfield Village)

NOVEMBER 3

A happy President Harry Truman displays the premature announcement of his defeat. (UPI/Bettmann Newsphotos)

A Mathew Brady photograph of General Winfield Scott, "Old Fuss and Feathers," a Virginian whom the Confederates hoped would join their cause. (Library of Congress)

broadcasting with reports of election returns. **1947** The *Spruce Goose,* Howard Hughes' 200-ton wooden flying boat, takes off on its only flight.

✦ **3** ✦

1623 The Dutch decide to set up a permanent colony in New Netherlands, and the Dutch West India Company prepares a detailed plan of government. **1948** "Dewey Defeats Truman," reads the front page headline of the *Chicago Daily Tribune,* based on premature election returns and the forecast of pollsters that New York governor Thomas Dewey would become the next president. **1966** President Lyndon B. Johnson signs a Truth-in-Packaging law that requires manufacturers of prepared foods to identify the ingredients on the label.

✦ **4** ✦

1646 The Massachusetts Bay Colony, feeling threatened by the arrival of Quakers, Baptists, and other claimants to liberty of conscience, makes heresy punishable by death. **1862** Richard J. Gatling receives a patent for his machine gun. He would write of the device: "It bears the same relation to other firearms that McCormack's reaper does to the sickle, or the sewing machine to the common needle." **1879** James Ritty receives a patent for the cash register, which is first thought of as a way to control pilferage by employees. **1979** Sixty-six Americans are taken hostage in the U.S. Embassy in Teheran by militant Shiite Muslims who demand the return from the United States of the deposed Shah.

NOVEMBER 5
Susan B. Anthony, an engraving from a photograph. (Library of Congress)

✦ 5 ✦

1830 Former President John Quincy Adams, defeated for re-election by Andrew Jackson, wins election to the House of Representatives. "My election as president of the United States was not half as gratifying," he writes in his diary. "No election or appointment conferred upon me ever gave me so much pleasure." **1872** Four days after she led a march to Rochester's city hall to demand that she be registered to vote, Susan B. Anthony defies the law by casting a ballot in a New York election.

✦ 6 ✦

1864 Southern diarist Mary Chesnut writes of home life in the waning days of the Civil War: "A thousand dollars has slipped through my fingers already this week. At the commissaries I spent five hundred today for sugar, candles, a lamp, &c. When the chimney of the lamp cracks, we plaster up the place with paper, thick letter paper, preferring the highly glazed kind. In that hunt queer old letters come to light." **1869** Rutgers beats Princeton, 6 to 4, in the first intercollegiate football game. There are twenty-five men on each team, and the rules do not permit running with the ball.

✦ 7 ✦

1775 Lord Dunmore, until the Revolution the royal governor of Virginia, offers to liberate male slaves who join the British army against the rebels. Within a few days over 800 slaves are recruited. **1841** Slaves being transported from Virginia to New Orleans aboard the *Creole* mutiny and take the ship into the British port of Nassau, where they are granted freedom.

NOVEMBER 5

A daguerreotype of Congressman John Quincy Adams, shortly before his death in 1848. This is the first photograph of a man who had held the office of president of the United States. (Metropolitan Museum of Art, Phelps Stokes Collection)

NOVEMBER 7

A button from each of Franklin D. Roosevelt's campaigns for the presidency. (Museum of American Political Life, University of Hartford)

1876 The presidential election ends in an electoral tie between Democrat Samuel J. Tilden and Republican Rutherford B. Hayes despite a huge popular majority for Tilden. The decision goes to the House, which does not resolve the matter until Inauguration Day, March 3, when Hayes is declared the winner—the result, it is said, of a deal between Southern Democrats and the Republicans, who agree to end Reconstruction in the South. **1944** President Franklin D. Roosevelt wins an unprecedented fourth term.

✦ 8 ✦

1880 Celebrated French actress Sarah Bernhardt makes her American debut at the age of thirty-six in Dumas Fils's *La Dame aux Camélias*. It is the first of ten American visits for Bernhardt, most of which are billed as farewell tours. **1889** Montana becomes the forty-first state to be admitted to the Union. **1910** The U.S. Congress has a Democratic majority for the first time since 1894. New members also include Victor Berger of Wisconsin, the first Socialist Congressman, who will be barred in 1918 and 1920 for his antiwar views, though later reelected. **1929** The Museum of Modern Art opens in New York City.

✦ 9 ✦

1872 A fire sweeping through Boston becomes catastrophic because a devastating equine virus, the Great Epizootic, has decimated the city's horses and immobilized the fire department. **1928** Anthropologist Margaret Mead arrives in Ta'u, Samoa, to begin research for her book *Coming of Age in Samoa,* which will influence the way generations of Americans view child-rearing practices. **1935** An aggressive group of labor leaders, including John L. Lewis of the Mine Workers and Sidney Hillman of the Amalgamated Clothing Workers, breaks away from the staid American Federation of Labor and forms the Committee for Industrial Organization (CIO), renamed the Congress of Industrial Organizations in 1938. **1965** When a Canadian generating plant near Niagara Falls suffers a failure, a blackout covers most of the Northeast, leaving more than 30 million people without electricity for over twelve hours.

✦ 10 ✦

1775 The Continental Congress creates the Marine Corps as a division of the Navy. **1782** King George III writes to the Earl of Shelburne about the Empire's recent loss: "I cannot conclude without mentioning how sensibly I feel the dismemberment of America from this empire, and that I should be miserable indeed if I did not feel that no blame on that account can be laid at my door, and did I not also know that knavery seems to be so much the striking feature of its inhabitants that it may not in the end be an evil that they will become aliens to this kingdom." **1865** Captain Henry Wirz, commandant of the notorious Confederate prisoner of war camp at Andersonville, Georgia, is executed after being tried for allowing mistreatment of Union soldiers during the Civil War.

NOVEMBER 11
Louis Armstrong and His Hot Five in Chicago, 1925. From left to right: Armstrong, Johnny St. Cyr, Johnny Dodds, Kid Ory, and Lil Hardin Armstrong, the leader's wife. (Frank Driggs Collection)

VEMBER 11
ilde Hassam captured the trium-
ant mood of the final weeks of
orld War I in *Avenue of the Allies,
at Britain, 1918,* which shows New
rk's Fifth Avenue decorated with
ied flags for a Liberty Loan drive.
Metropolitan Museum of Art)

✦ 11 ✦

1865 Mary Edward Walker, the first female surgeon in the U.S. Army and a Confederate prisoner of war for four months, becomes the only woman to be awarded the Medal of Honor. The award is revoked by a review board but restored posthumously. **1882** Influential social theorist Herbert Spencer, invoking a new leisure ethic for the prosperous, tells a banquet audience in New York City, "We have had somewhat too much of the 'gospel of work.'" **1889** Washington is admitted to the Union as the forty-second state. **1918** Armistice Day brings the end of World War I. **1925** Louis Armstrong goes into a studio to record the first of his Hot Five recordings, which transform him from a local legend in New Orleans and Chicago to the leading exponent of a new, uniquely American music. **1932** The Tomb of the Unknown Soldier is dedicated in Arlington, Virginia.

✦ 12 ✦

1766 John Singleton Copley writes to Benjamin West to lament the condition of art in America: "In this Country as you rightly observe, there is no examples of Art, except what is to be met with in a few prints, indifferently exicuted, from which it is impossible to learn much." **1946** The Exchange National Bank of Chicago opens the world's first drive-in bank.

✦ 13 ✦

1749 Twenty-four Philadelphia residents, inspired by Benjamin Franklin's writing on the value of education, form an academy with Franklin as president of the board of trustees. Out of this institution will grow the nation's first nonsectarian college, the University of Pennsylvania. **1839** Abolitionists hold a political convention in Warsaw, New York, and create the Liberty Party, nominating James G. Birney, a former slaveowner from Kentucky, to run for president. **1927** The Holland Tunnel, under the Hudson River between Jersey City, New Jersey, and New York City, opens to traffic, the nation's first underwater tunnel for vehicles. **1956** The Supreme Court, reviewing a Montgomery, Alabama law, rules that segregation on interstate buses is unconstitutional.

OVEMBER 16

Pack Train to Santa Fe, 1820, by *ederic* Remington. (From Henry *man's* book, *The Old Santa Fe Trail*)

✦ 14 ✦

1887 Thomas Edison, in a letter describing his latest workshop, this one in West Orange, New Jersey, touches on another of his innovations, the research laboratory: "Inventions that formerly took months and cost a large sum can now be done in 2 or 3 days with very small expense, as I shall carry a stock of almost every conceivable material of every size and with the latest machinery a man will produce 10 times as much as in a laboratory which has but little material." **1961** President John F. Kennedy decides to increase the number of American advisers in Vietnam from 1,000 to 16,000 over the next two years.

✦ 15 ✦

1777 While the War of Independence is still being fought, the Continental Congress adopts "Articles of Confederation and Perpetual Union" as a basis for government, assigning one vote to each state, and requiring a vote of 9 out of 13 to create legislation or a unanimous vote to amend the document. The Articles do not provide for a chief executive. **1864** General William T. Sherman begins his 300-mile march of destruction across Georgia to the sea. **1904** King Camp Gillette receives a patent for a razor with disposable blades. **1969** In the largest antiwar demonstration in U.S. history, an estimated 250,000 people march in Washington, D.C., to protest the war in Vietnam.

✦ 16 ✦

1798 In a demonstration of continuing enmity British sailors board the *Baltimore,* an American frigate, allegedly seeking Royal Navy deserters. They seize several *Baltimore* crew members, creating the sort of incident that will lead to the War of 1812. **1821** Pioneer trader William Becknell reaches Santa Fe ten weeks after departing Independence, Missouri, and proves that his route, which becomes the Santa Fe Trail, is faster than the traditional trail from Mexico City. **1884** Samuel S. McClure establishes the first major newspaper syndicate service, based on the telegraph and a network of field correspondents that originated during the Civil War. Reliance on the telegraph, observed a writer, has "made all the leading papers so nearly alike as to their news that one does not differ in that respect materially from the others." **1907** Oklahoma is admitted to the Union as the forty-sixth state. **1933** Sixteen years after the end of the Russian Revolution, the United States and the Soviet Union establish diplomatic relations.

EGIN EARLY   SHAVE YOURSELF
Gillette Safety NO STROPPING NO HONING **Razor**

VEMBER 15

1905 advertisement for the Gillette *ety* Razor, the year after Gillette *n* his patent. (Bryan Holme)

✦ 17 ✦

1800 Congress convenes in Washington for the first time, sixteen days after President and Mrs. John Adams move into the new official residence built on a bog, with no bathrooms or water supply. **1858** William Larimer, a Pennsylvania businessman who went broke in the depression of 1854, founds a settlement, to be called Denver, near Pike's Peak, across a creek from where Colorado's first settlers have pitched tents. "We shall have a good hotel here by spring," Larimer writes to his wife. **1875** The immigrant Russian psychic, Madame Blavatsky, founds an American branch of the Theosophical Society in New York. **1880** The Chinese Exclusion Treaty, signed in Peking, gives the United States the right to "regulate, limit, or suspend" immigrants from China but not exclude them entirely.

✦ 18 ✦

1751 The *South Carolina Gazette* advertises the services of Anna Maria Hoyland, who does "any kind of braziery, and tin work as her mother used to do." **1861** The day after hearing Union soldiers singing *John Brown's Body Lies A-Mouldering in the Grave,* Boston poet Julia Ward Howe writes *The Battle Hymn of the Republic* to the tune. The composer of the traditional melody, an old camp-meeting tune, is unknown. **1883** Congress divides the nation into standard time zones according to a system devised by the railroads for their timetables. **1903** The United States and Panama sign the Hay-Buneau-Varilla Treaty, which gives the United States the right to construct a canal and per-

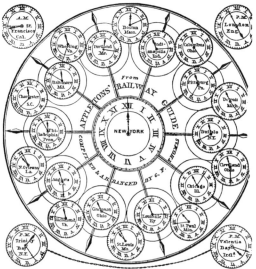

UNITED STATES TIME INDICATOR,

NOVEMBER 18

A timetable from mid-nineteenth century, before the railroads established standardized time zones.

NOVEMBER 20
The wreck of the *Essex,* an incident that impressed the nation with the vengeful powers of a sperm whale. "He came down on us with full speed and struck the ship with his head," wrote one of the survivors. "The ship brought up as suddenly and violently as if she had struck a rock and trembled for a few seconds like a leaf." (Forbes Collection, Hart Nautical Collections, MIT Museum)

manent rights to a ten-mile strip of Panama in return for $10 million and an annual fee of $250,000 after nine years. **1978** Representative Leo Ryan of California and others are killed while investigating an American religious cult based in Jonestown, Guyana. The next day, acting on the orders of their leader, the Reverend Jim Jones, 911 members of the group commit mass suicide.

✦ 19 ✦

1831 James A. Garfield, the twentieth president of the United States, is born in Orange Township, Ohio. "My God, what is there in this place that a man would ever want to get into it?" he said of the White House. **1863** President Abraham Lincoln and Edward Everett deliver speeches at the dedication of a military cemetery on the site of the Gettysburg battlefield in Pennsylvania. The speech by Everett, the most celebrated orator of his day, is by far the more acclaimed, while Lincoln's remarks are so brief that they make little impression. One newspaper reported that a speech "more dull and commonplace it would not be easy to produce." **1919** The U.S. Senate fails to ratify the Treaty of Versailles, thus crushing President Wilson's hope for American international leadership in the post-World War I world. **1945** President Harry S. Truman, trying to carry on the social agenda of Franklin Roosevelt, asks Congress to create a program of national health insurance.

✦ 20 ✦

1820 The *Essex* of Nantucket, hunting whales in the Pacific, is rammed and sunk by an enraged sperm whale. When the eight survivors are rescued, after ninety-six days at sea, their tales of the attack and aftermath, in which the men resorted to cannibalism, make the wreck the most famous whaling disaster of the century. **1894** *Prince Ananias,* the first operetta by Victor Herbert, most popular composer of the musical theater of his time, opens in New York. **1919** The country's first municipal airport opens in Tuscon, Arizona. **1969** The Department of Agriculture bans the insecticide DDT in residential areas.

NOVEMBER 22
Moments after the assassination of
President John F. Kennedy in Dallas.
(UPI/Bettmann Newsphotos)

✦ 21 ✦

1620 In Provincetown Harbor forty-one adult males aboard the *Mayflower* sign an agreement (known after 1793 as the Mayflower Compact) pledging the colonists to "covenant and combine our selves togeather into a civille body politick." The passengers then disembark and, after preliminary investigation, decide that Provincetown is unsuitable for colonization and set sail again to explore a likelier spot along Cape Cod. **1789** North Carolina ratifies the Constitution and becomes the twelfth state. **1925** Harold E. "Red" Grange, the most acclaimed college football star of his era, plays his last game for the University of Illinois, days before he stirs nationwide controversy by signing a professional contract. **1974** Congress passes the Freedom of Information Act over President Ford's veto.

✦ 22 ✦

1963 President John F. Kennedy is fatally shot at midday in Dallas, Texas, where he had gone on a political fence-mending trip. The president was riding in an open motorcade with his wife and Texas Governor John Connally (who was also shot but not fatally). In the next few hours Vice President Lyndon B. Johnson takes the oath of office aboard Air Force One, the presidential plane, and police arrest Lee Harvey Oswald, a former U.S. Marine sharpshooter who had lived in the Soviet Union, and charge him with the murder. **1972** The State Department ends a 22-year ban on travel to mainland China.

✦ 23 ✦

1804 Franklin Pierce, fourteenth president of the United States, is born in Hillsborough, New Hampshire. A college classmate and friend of Nathaniel Hawthorne, Pierce would be known as a "doughface," a Northerner with Southern principles, and in foreign policy would be remembered for his desire to acquire Cuba as a slave state. **1903** Italian opera star Enrico Caruso, perhaps the first singer whose voice becomes famous through recordings, makes his American debut at the Metropolitan Opera House. **1945** The government ends the rationing of all foods except sugar.

✦ 24 ✦

1784 Zachary Taylor, twelfth president of the United States, is born in Orange Court House, Virginia. Renowned for his informality, President Taylor inspired one observer to remark, "He looks more like an old farmer going to market with eggs than anything I can think of." **1832** Sectional conflict reaches new intensity when South Carolina passes a law nullifying federal tariff measures within the state. President Andrew Jackson calls a military alert after issuing a proclamation affirming the supremacy of the federal government, but a compromise is reached the following spring, and both sides claim victory. **1865** Mississippi passes the Black Codes, which forbid blacks to serve on juries, testify against whites, bear arms, hold large meetings, or attend white schools. **1874** Joseph Glidden receives a patent for barbed wire, which, once accepted as fencing material, makes possible the development of the Great Plains for farming. **1904** In New York, Alfred Stieglitz and Edward Steichen open 291, the first gallery to exhibit photography as a fine art.

NOVEMBER 22

Lyndon Johnson sworn in as president aboard Air Force One, flanked by Lady Bird Johnson, left, and Jacqueline Kennedy, right. (UPI/Bettmann Newsphotos)

✦ 25 ✦

1758 A British force that includes woodsman Daniel Boone captures Fort Duquesne from the French and renames it Pittsburgh. **1795** Benjamin Henry Latrobe leaves England to settle in the United States, where, as the nation's first professional architect, he will supervise construction of the Capitol Building and then rebuild it after the British invasion of Washington in 1812. **1864** In a production of *Julius Caesar* at New York's Winter Garden the three Booth brothers appear together on stage for the only time. **1869** The *New York Weekly* announces the serialization of "Buffalo Bill, the King of the Border Men," by Ned Buntline, a dime novelist who had gone out west in search of an authentic western hero and found William Cody among cavalry scouts in Nebraska. **1915** The Ku Klux Klan, a vigilante society which was formed during Reconstruction and subsequently fell into disrepute even among diehard Confederates, is revived in Atlanta. **1969** President Richard Nixon orders the destruction of germ warfare stockpiles.

✦ 26 ✦

1789 A proclamation by President Washington declares Thanksgiving Day a national holiday, in part to give thanks for the nation's new Constitution. The proclamation is denounced

NOVEMBER 25

The Booth brothers on stage: left to right, John Wilkes as noble Marc Antony, Edwin as Brutus, and Junius as Cassius. (Theatre Collection, Harvard College Library)

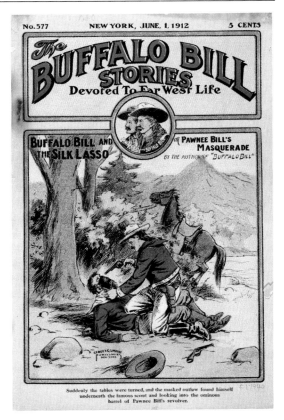

No. 577   NEW YORK, JUNE, 1, 1912   5 CENTS

The **BUFFALO BILL STORIES**
Devoted To Far West Life

BUFFALO BILL AND THE SILK LASSO   *or* PAWNEE BILL'S MASQUERADE
BY THE AUTHOR OF "BUFFALO BILL"

Suddenly the tables were turned, and the masked outlaw found himself underneath the famous scout and looking into the ominous barrel of Pawnee Bill's revolver.

as a violation of states' rights by opponents of the Constitution and foes of the Federalist Party. **1832** In New York City public service begins on the nation's first streetcar, a thirty-passenger horse-drawn car with iron wheels pulled over iron rails. **1941** A Japanese carrier force leaves its bases and heads toward Pearl Harbor.

✦ 27 ✦

1755 Joseph Salvador buys 100,000 acres near Fort Ninety-six in South Carolina for the first Jewish settlement in the colonies. His grandson, Francis Salvador, will be the first Jew elected to public office in America. **1941** The commander of the Army's Hawaiian department receives a coded message from General Marshall: "Negotiations with Japan appear to be terminated to all practical purposes . . . . future action unpredictable but hostile action possible at any moment. If hostilities cannot, repeat cannot be avoided the United States desires that Japan commit the first overt act. . . . Measures should be carried out so as not, repeat not, to alarm civil population or disclose intent."

NOVEMBER 30

The American representatives at the preliminary peace negotiations with Britain. From left: John Jay, John Adams, Benjamin Franklin, Henry Laurens, and Temple Franklin, grandson of Benjamin. The painter Benjamin West left space for the British commissioners, but they refused to sit for him. (Henry Francis du Pont Winterthur Museum)

✦ 28 ✦

1520 In the course of the first circumnavigation of the earth, Ferdinand Magellan reaches the Pacific Ocean and names it Mare Pacificum. **1844** Diarist Philip Hone notes that he never opens a newspaper that does not contain reports of disasters involving railroads or steamboats: "This world is going on too fast. Improvements, Politics, Reform, Religion—all fly. Railroads, steamers, packets, race against time and beat it hollow. Flying is dangerous. By and by we shall have balloons and pass over to Europe between sun and sun. Oh, for the good old days of heavy post-coaches and speed at the rate of six miles an hour." **1895** In the nation's first automobile race, two electrical-powered and four gasoline-driven cars race from Chicago to Evanston and back, the winner averaging 7 mph. **1942** Americans are temporarily distracted from war news by reports of a fire at the Cocoanut Grove, a Boston nightclub, where artificial decor ignites and creates carbon monoxide in an establishment that lacks ventilation and adequate emergency exists. In twelve minutes, 492 people receive fatal injuries.

✦ 29 ✦

1775 The Committee on Secret Correspondence, a forerunner of the State Department, is created by the revolutionaries to sound out potential European allies against the British. **1780** Lemuel Haynes, a Revolutionary War veteran, receives a license to preach in the Congregational Church, becoming the first black preacher licensed by a white church. In 1785, an appointment to the Congregational Church of Torrington, Connecticut, will make him the first black pastor of a white church. And in 1804, Middlebury College in Vermont will award Haynes the first degree from an American college to a black. **1890** In the first Army–Navy football game, held at West Point, New York, Navy shuts out Army, 24–0.

✦ 30 ✦

1755 Nine hundred neutral French arrive in Maryland, exiled from their home in Acadia (Nova Scotia) by the British Army, which regards them as spies. Some Acadians will eventually return home despite continuing hostility, but many settle permanently in French-speaking Louisiana, where "Acadian" has become shortened to "Cajun." **1782** The United States and Britain sign a provisional treaty ending the Revolution, to be followed by the Treaty of Paris the following year. The provisional treaty stipulates that former supporters of the British should be immune from further property confiscations or other persecution. The American signatories are John Adams, Benjamin Franklin, John Jay, and Henry Laurens.

December

✦ 1 ✦

1824 In the presidential contest between dour John Quincy Adams and flamboyant Andrew Jackson, neither candidate wins a majority of electoral votes. By the terms of the 12th Amendment, the matter goes to the House of Representatives, where Adams is voted president on February 9, 1825. **1955** Rosa Parks, a seamstress and NAACP member in Montgomery, Alabama, tests the city's racial segregation laws when she refuses to give up her seat to a white man on a city bus. "I was just tired from shopping. I had my sacks and all, and my feet hurt." She is arrested and, four days later, fined $10 for violating public transportation laws. By that time, a boycott of the bus system has been organized with the help of the twenty-seven-year-old pastor of Dexter Avenue Baptist Church, Dr. Martin Luther King, Jr.

✦ 2 ✦

1823 President James Monroe sends a foreign policy statement to Congress that becomes known as the Monroe Doctrine: "The American continents, by the free and independent condition which they have assumed and maintained, are henceforth not to be considered as subjects for future colonization by any European powers." **1845** President James Polk's first annual message to Congress elaborates on the Monroe Doctrine: "The people of *this continent alone* have the right to decide their own destiny." **1942** Enrico Fermi and his associates produce the first self-sustaining nuclear chain reaction at their laboratory in a converted squash-rackets court at the University of Chicago. **1982** Sixty-two-year-old Barney C. Clarke becomes the first human recipient of an artificial heart in an operation at the University of Utah Medical Center.

✦ 3 ✦

1775 The first official American flag is raised aboard the naval vessel *Alfred.* The flag has thirteen red and white stripes with the crosses of St. George and St. Andrew. **1818** Illinois is admitted to the Union as the twenty-first state with its first capital at Kaskaskia. **1838** Joshua R. Giddings of Ohio becomes the first active abolitionist to be elected to Congress. In 1841, Giddings will resign after being interrupted and censured for a speech. Reelected to Congress, he returns and completes his speech. **1868** With Supreme Court Chief Justice Salmon Chase presiding in Richmond, the treason trial of former Confederate President Jefferson Davis opens. The chief justice, formerly Lincoln's secretary of the treasury, will cooperate with President Andrew Johnson in delaying the proceedings until a general amnesty for Confederates is proclaimed the following February 15.

DECEMBER 24 *(Opening illustration)*
In *Exhumation of the Mastodon,* Charles Willson Peale commemorates his paleontological labors and contributes to the debate over whether the New World was really newer than the Old World. (Peale Museum, Baltimore)

DECEMBER 4
In one of the Thomas Nast cartoons that helped bring down Boss Tweed, the boss and his cohorts are pictured as vultures who picked clean the bones of New York. (Culver Pictures)

DECEMBER 4

Granger meeting, Scott County, Illinois, 1873. One placard reads: "President $50,000 a Year, Congressmen $7000 a Year, Farmers 75 cts. a Week?" (Library of Congress)

1674 The Jesuit missionary Jacques Marquette builds a mission house, the first building on the site of the trading post that will become the city of Chicago. **1867** Oliver Hudson Kelley resigns from a job at the Agriculture Department to form the Patrons of Husbandry, a secret society that soon becomes known as the Grange, after a word for meeting places. The organization grows to 858,000 members within six years and begins to wield political power in strong farm states. **1875** William Marcy "Boss" Tweed, the toppled political czar and leader of New York's Tammany Hall organization, escapes the Ludlow Street jail where he was serving a twelve-year sentence for fraud. He flees to Cuba and is captured in Spain in November 1876.

The fleet at Pearl Harbor under attack. From left, the *West Virginia,* the *Tennessee,* and the *Arizona.* Today the *Arizona* still lies under the harbor with most of its crew. (National Archives)

✦ 5 ✦

1791 Secretary of Treasury Alexander Hamilton presents his *Report on Manufactures* to Congress. It urges government to take a strong hand in nurturing trade, countering the advice of those like Thomas Jefferson who associate manufacturing with corruption. Hamilton also observes: "It is worthy of particular remark that in general women and children are rendered more useful, and the latter more easily useful, by manufacturing establishments than they otherwise would be." **1865** The steel industry is transformed when Sir Henry Bessemer receives an American patent for his method of converting iron to steel by blowing air through molten iron to remove impurities. The process makes it possible to use steel where it would have been too expensive before—in making steel rails, for example, which are produced in Chicago in time to be used in building the transcontinental railroad.

✦ 6 ✦

1790 Congress moves from New York City to Philadelphia until its permanent new home in the federal district on the Potomac is ready. **1825** President John Quincy Adams is widely ridiculed, and his political reputation permanently damaged, by his First Annual Message to Congress, which recommends government support of scientific research, establishment of a national university, and sponsorship of an astronomical observatory. **1891** Park designer Frederick Law Olmsted, retained by George Vanderbilt, hires Gifford Pinchot

CEMBER 8
esident Roosevelt signs the declara-
on of war. (Library of Congress)

ECEMBER 8
eadlines draw passersby in San
rancisco. (National Archives)

as forester for the Biltmore Estate, Vanderbilt's 6,000 wooded acres in South Carolina, a "museum of living trees" whose budget is larger than that of the U.S. Agriculture Department.

✦ 7 ✦

1787 Delaware is the first to ratify the new plan of government and thus earns its nickname "First State of the Union." **1796** President Washington urges Congress to direct its efforts and government money to aiding agriculture: "To what object can it be dedicated with greater propriety?" **1941** Military cryptographers in Washington interpret Japanese diplomatic messages to mean that an attack in the Pacific is imminent, and a warning telegraph is sent to Pearl Harbor, where, because it is Sunday, the communications network is closed. As a messenger on a bicycle approaches naval headquarters, the first of 360 Japanese planes reaches the harbor.

✦ 8 ✦

1886 The American Federation of Labor organizes as a federation of craft unions with one full-time officer—President Samuel Gompers, a former cigar maker who describes the organization's goals as "more and more, here and now." **1941** Stunned by the surprise attack on Pearl Harbor, the United States declares war on Japan, but not on Germany or Italy. Their declarations of war bring the United States into the European war on December 11.

✦ 9 ✦

1502 King Henry VII grants a patent of exploration to a group of English and Portuguese merchants called the Company of Adventurers to the New World. **1775** The war comes to Virginia: In the first encounter between British and rebels since Bunker Hill, Colonel William Woodford's militia defeat Lord Dunmore's troops at Great Bridge near Norfolk. **1803** Congress passes the Twelfth Amendment, providing for separate ballots for electing the president and vice president and outlining an order of succession if no candidate wins a majority. **1889** The Chicago Auditorium, a landmark building designed by Louis Sullivan and his partner and mentor, Dankmar Adler, opens to the public. Assisting on the project is the young Frank Lloyd Wright, who had been hired to help with the drawings.

✦ 10 ✦

1607 Captain John Smith of the Jamestown colony goes off on a food-finding mission, which leads to his capture by Indians and rescue by Pocahontas, daughter of Chief Powhatan. **1653** Dutch and English settlers near the New Amsterdam settlement meet to protest the autocratic governing methods of the colony's owners, the Dutch West India Company. **1817** Mississippi is admitted to the Union as the twentieth state. **1832** Reacting to South Carolina's attempt to nullify the tariff laws within its borders, President Andrew Jackson reinforces Fort Sumter and warns the state that secession would not be tolerated. **1869** The Territory of Wyoming grants women the right to vote.

✦ 11 ✦

1776 The Continental Congress grants General Washington extraordinary powers to take whatever he needs to equip the

DECEMBER 9

Louis Sullivan's design for the Chicago Auditorium abandoned the Victorian Gothic and Romanesque style for public buildings. (Richard Nickel

POWHATAN BRAND

DECEMBER 10

tobacco label tribute to the rescue John Smith by Pocahontas. "She azarded the beating out of her own rains to save mine," Smith wrote. library of Congress)

Army, by force if not obtainable at a reasonable price. But one Congress member, Charles Carroll of Carrollton, Maryland, wrote that the general "is so humane and delicate that I fear the common cause will suffer." **1816** Indiana is admitted to the Union as the nineteenth state with a constitution that represents a compromise between pro- and antislavery residents: Slavery is forbidden, but blacks are not allowed to vote or serve in the militia. **1882** The Bijou Theater in Boston presents the first theatrical performance illuminated by incandescent electric lights. For a performance of Gilbert and Sullivan's *Iolanthe,* 650 bulbs are used. **1961** Two U.S. Army helicopter companies, representing the first direct military support for South Vietnam, arrive in Saigon.

✦ 12 ✦

1787 Pennsylvania ratifies the Constitution and becomes the second state of the Union. **1792** The First Bank of the United States, conceived by Treasury Secretary Alexander Hamilton as the fiscal agent for the government, opens its main office in Philadelphia, over the objections of Thomas Jefferson that the Constitution doesn't provide the government with the power to create a national bank. **1870** Joseph R. Rainey of South Carolina is sworn in as the first black member of the House of Representatives. **1937** Japanese planes attack and sink the U.S. gunboat *Panay* on the Yangtze River in China. The Japanese government apologizes and offers to pay indemnity.

✦ 13 ✦

1816 The nation's first savings bank, the Provident Institution for Savings, opens in Boston. By 1819 the practice of paying interest on deposits appears in New York, Philadelphia, and Baltimore. **1862** At the Battle of Fredericksburg, General Ambrose Burnside's Army of the Potomac launches virtually suicidal assaults up Marye's Hill. Watching the one-sided slaughter, General Lee remarked, "It is well that war is so terrible; men would love it too much."

✦ 14 ✦

1774 After a warning from Paul Revere that British troops would be posted at Portsmouth, New Hampshire, Major John Sullivan leads a patriot raid on Fort William and Mary in Portsmouth and carries off a supply of guns and powder—the first military action of the American Revolution. **1799** George Washington, aged sixty-seven, dies at his home in Mount Vernon after falling ill and being bled by his doctors. **1819** Alabama, separated from Mississippi only two years before, is admitted to the Union as the twenty-second state. **1894** Socialist leader Eugene Debs is sentenced to a six-month jail term for his role in a sympathy strike of railroad workers during the Pullman company strike. Debs's lawyer, handling his first big case, is Clarence Darrow.

DECEMBER 14

Eugene Debs, seated at far left, posing in 1870 with fellow workers at the Terre Haute and Indianapolis Railroad shop yard. (Eugene V. Debs Foundation)

The Boston Tea Party was carried out without resistance, although the harbor was full of armed British ships. (Library of Congress)

✦ **15** ✦

1792 Over the objections of Patrick Henry, who considered its protections too weak, Virginia approves the Bill of Rights, thereby completing the ratification process for the first ten amendments to the Constitution. **1948** Former State Department official Alger Hiss is indicted for perjury after denying that he passed on secret government documents to journalist Whittaker Chambers, then a Communist agent. **1973** The American Psychiatric Association reverses its traditional position and declares that homosexuality is not a mental illness.

✦ **16** ✦

1773 At the Boston Tea Party thirty to sixty men board three merchant ships and empty their tea chests overboard, making Boston harbor a "teapot." The East India Company will ask only that its losses be made good, but Parliament responds soon with the "Intolerable Acts," which close the port and increase the powers of the royal governor. **1811** An earthquake shatters the thinly settled valley of the Ohio and Mississippi rivers, comparable in magnitude to the San Francisco earthquake of 1906 but not in cost; only two lives were lost. The steamboat *New Orleans,* making the pioneer journey down the Mississippi, is jolted by the quake but continues on course. **1944** American forces in the Ardennes Forest in Belgium are taken by surprise by a powerful German attack, which creates a salient of resistance in the retreating American line. Thus this last-gasp attempt by the Germans to stave off defeat earned the name Battle of the Bulge.

✦ 17 ✦

1777 While General William Howe quarters his troops in Philadelphia for the winter, General Washington takes his army to Valley Forge, a defensible hilly area eighteen miles northwest of the city, and sets the men to constructing huts. Food is scarce, clothing is scarce, and there is no water nearby. **1903** Near Kitty Hawk, North Carolina, Wilbur and Orville Wright take their 745-pound, 12-horsepower plane into the air. At the end of the day Orville sends a telegram to their father in Dayton, Ohio, where the brothers operated a bicycle shop: "SUCCESS FOUR FLIGHTS THURSDAY MORNING ALL AGAINST TWENTY ONE MILE WIND STARTED FROM LEVEL WITH ENGINE POWER ALONE AVERAGE SPEED THROUGH AIR THIRTY ONE MILES LONGEST 57 SECONDS INFORM PRESS HOME FOR CHRISTMAS." The air age had begun.

✦ 18 ✦

1787 New Jersey ratifies the Constitution and becomes the third state of the Union. **1789** In accord with the new Constitution, which spells out the terms for creating new states, Virginia releases Kentucky Territory from its jurisdiction. Under the Articles of Confederation individual states had treated unorganized territory as extensions of their own domains. **1837** "A change of clothes is all we want," writes Mary Richardson of Maine, in her journal after learning from her fiancé that they will be moving to Oregon as foreign missionaries. "Buckskin drawers are the best for riding on horseback.

Our ladies should also have drawers to prevent being chafted in riding. We should carry no baggage excepting such as we want to wear or use on the journey."

✦ 19 ✦

1732 The Pennsylvania *Gazette* announces the publication of a new enterprise by Benjamin Franklin, writing under the name Richard Saunders: "POOR RICHARD: AN ALMANACK containing the Lunations, Eclipses, Planets Motions and Aspects, Weather, Sun and Moon's rising and setting, Highwater &c. besides many pleasant and witty Verses, Jests and Sayings, Author's Motive of Writing . . . by Richard Saunders, Philomat." **1911** A group of artists trying to break away from the influence of the conservative Academy of Design, including the painter George Bellows and sculptor Jo Davidson, organizes the Association of American Sculptors and Painters. The general public will first hear of the group when it launches the Armory Show of modern art in 1913.

✦ 20 ✦

1790 Samuel Slater, who memorized exclusive British technology for spinning machines and came to America with the plans in his head, launches America's cotton industry with a water-powered mill at Pawtucket, Rhode Island. Slater also pioneered the use of child labor in his factories. **1820** Missouri imposes a $1 per year bachelor's tax on unmarried men between twenty-one and fifty. **1860** While the rest of the nation waits to see what changes newly elected President Lincoln will bring, South Carolina holds a convention that votes to secede from the Union.

✦ **21** ✦

1620 The settlers aboard the *Mayflower*, who have been cruising the coast of Cape Cod in search of a suitable site for their colony, weigh anchor at Plymouth, and an exploring party comes ashore—first setting foot, it is said, on Plymouth Rock. **1850** The Hungarian chargé d'affaires protests the moral support the United States has been expressing for Hungarian revolutionaries. Secretary of State Daniel Webster defends the nation's involvement when "events appeared to have their origin in those great ideas . . . on which the American constitutions themselves are founded." **1937** *Snow White and the Seven Dwarfs*, Walt Disney's first full-length animated film, opens in Los Angeles.

✦ **22** ✦

1775 The Continental Congress establishes a four-ship Navy, although it proves to be of little help in fighting for independence, and most of the Americans' gains at sea are achieved by privateers. **1847** Congressman Abraham Lincoln of Illinois makes his first speech in the House, a bitter denunciation of President Polk and the Mexican War in which he calls the president "a bewildered, confounded and miserably perplexed man." Polk and the war are popular back home, and the speech is a disaster for Lincoln, who will not run for reelection.

✦ 23 ✦

1788 Maryland offers a ten-square mile tract on the Potomac River as the site of a federal district to house the national government. **1852** The first train to run west of the Mississippi travels five miles from St. Louis to Cheltenham, a modest beginning on building plans that have aimed toward a transcontinental railroad ever since gold was discovered in California in 1848. **1947** A team of Bell Laboratories physicists under William Shockley invents the transistor as a replacement for vacuum tubes. **1973** Heralding a revolution in professional baseball, labor arbitrator Peter M. Seitz rules that a player cannot be bound indefinitely to one team without his consent. Seitz rules that Andy Messersmith and Dave McNally, two pitchers who had been playing without contracts, are now "free agents" who can sell their services to any team.

✦ 24 ✦

1801 Charles Willson Peale, artist, pioneer paleontologist, and friend of Thomas Jefferson, exhibits a mounted skeleton of a mastodon to members of the American Philosophical Society at Philadelphia. **1851** A fire at the Library of Congress destroys two thirds of the collection. **1948** A solar heating system designed by Dr. Maria Telkes is installed in a house in Dover, Massachusetts.

DECEMBER 22
The earliest known photograph of Abraham Lincoln, probably made in 1846, from a daguerreotype thought to have been made by N. H. Shepherd in Springfield, Illinois. (Library of Congress)

✦ 25 ✦

1620 Governor Bradford reports that the colonists at Plymouth worked at building houses—"no man rested all that day"—although he did order an issue of beer for the pilgrims. **1651** The Massachusetts General Court ordered a 5 shilling fine for anyone caught "observing any such day as Christmas." **1804** Christmas is celebrated at Fort Dearborn with a decorated fir tree, a German custom. **1804** From the *Journals of Lewis and Clark:* "we fired the Swivels at day break & each man fired one round. our officers Gave the party a drink of Taffee. we had the Best to eat that could be had, & continued dancing & frolicking dureing the whole day. the Savages did not Trouble us as we had requested them not to come as it was a Great medician day with us. We enjoyed a merry christmas dureing the day & evening until nine oClock—all in peace & quietness." **1831** Louisiana and Arkansas become the first states to observe Christmas as a legal holiday.

✦ 26 ✦

1776 At the Battle of Trenton, General Washington takes advantage of the enemy's Christmas celebrations to achieve a surprise victory. Having retreated across the Delaware to Pennsylvania a few weeks before, Washington recrossed the river into New Jersey on Christmas night and attacked early the next morning while the soldiers of the Trenton garrison, most of them German mercenaries, were sleeping off the previous day's festivities. **1865** Inventor James Nason of Franklin, Massachusetts, introduces his new creation, a percolator for brewing coffee.

✦ 27 ✦

1820 John Quincy Adams notes that the District of Columbia is a city lacking in monuments: "There is a resolution of Congress, existing ever since the death of Washington, that a monument in honor of his memory should be erected. . . . Congress ought to build a church of durable stone, equal in dimensions to Westminster Abbey or the Pantheon at Paris" in which the nation's heroes could be entombed. **1860** South Carolina raises the state flag at Castle Pinckney, the day after it is abandoned by federal troops, who withdraw to Fort Sumter in Charleston harbor. **1932** Radio City Music Hall, a monumental showplace that combines a live stage performance with movies, opens to an awed public.

DECEMBER 28
President Woodrow Wilson, here throwing out a ball to open the baseball season. (Library of Congress)

DECEMBER 25

A clean and merry Christmas from Old Dutch Cleanser—a sign that by the early twentieth century Christmas was also becoming a secular American holiday. *(Kitchen Arts & Letters)*

Paves the Way for Cleanliness and Good Cheer

A Merry Xmas and A Happy New Year

✦ 28 ✦

1832 Feeling betrayed by fellow Southerner Andrew Jackson, John C. Calhoun resigns as Jackson's vice president to carry on the fight for slavery and states rights as senator from South Carolina. **1846** Iowa is admitted to the Union as the twenty-ninth state. **1856** Woodrow Wilson, the twenty-eighth president of the United States, is born in Staunton, Virginia, the son of a Presbyterian minister. **1869** William F. Semple of Mount Vernon, Ohio, is awarded a patent for chewing gum.

✦ 29 ✦

1808 Andrew Johnson, who became seventeenth president upon the death of Abraham Lincoln, is born in Raleigh, North Carolina. **1837** The *Caroline,* an American steamboat carrying supplies to Canadian revolutionaries, is boarded on the Niagara River and set afire by Canadian militia, creating new tensions in a period of hostile relations between the United States and Britain. **1845** Texas becomes the twenty-eighth state to be admitted to the Union. **1851** The first YMCA in the United States opens its doors in Boston. **1890** At Wounded Knee Creek, South Dakota, the last skirmish is fought between American Indians and U.S. government forces—500 cavalrymen against 120 braves and 230 women and children. The Indians are virtually wiped out. **1913** The first movie serial, the thirteen-part *Adventures of Kathleen,* begins playing in Chicago.

✦ 30 ✦

1903 Fire breaks out in Chicago's Iroquois Theater, packed with an audience of women and children. Despite the efforts of comedian Eddie Foy to calm the crowd, hundreds are trapped by blocked exits, and 571 people are killed. In the aftermath, theater safety codes are tightened, and public buildings install doors that open outward. **1940** Los Angeles dedicates the Arroyo Seco Parkway, its first freeway. **1952** The Tuskegee Institute reports that 1952 was the first in 71 years that there were no lynchings in the United States.

✦ 31 ✦

1854 George Templeton Strong marks the passing of another year in a troubled, ominous decade: "There goes the clock, the old year is out, amid a fusillade from the distant German region, east of Tompkins Square, that sounds like the preliminary skirmish of a great battle . . ." **1904** A new tradition begins as crowds gather in New York's Times Square to celebrate the end of the old year. As midnight strikes, an illuminated globe descends a pole atop the Times Tower, ushering in the new year. **1935** The U.S. Patent Office issues a patent to Parker Brothers for the Depression-inspired game of Monopoly. **1943** Four hundred New York City police are called out to control the frenzied crowds as the young Frank Sinatra begins a singing engagement at the Paramount Theater.

DECEMBER 31
The crowds gather for the traditional New Year's Eve celebration in Times Square, 1946. (V. DePauw, © 1946, 1974, The New Yorker Magazine, Inc.)

A Note on This Book

A Note on the Research

One of the most basic facts about an event, the day it happened, is often among the most difficult to establish. Everyone agrees that Tom Paine wrote *Common Sense,* but experts disagree about the day it was published. Whenever possible, we consulted source documents such as contemporary letters, journals, legislative records or newspapers to establish the dates of the events in *A Book of Days in American History.* In other cases we joined what seemed to be the consensus among authorities. And we consulted many historical chronologies and almanacs, particularly those listed below:

The Dictionary of Dates by Helen Rex Keller, vol. 2, *The New World* (New York: Macmillan, 1934).

The Encyclopedia of American Facts and Dates by Gorton Carruth, fifth ed. (New York: T. Y. Crowell, 1970) and eighth ed. (New York: Harper & Row, 1987).

The Encyclopedia of American History edited by Richard B. Morris (New York: Harper & Row, 1976).

A Note on the Calendar

Any attempt to record the dates of events in Colonial American history is made even more difficult by the change in the calendar that occurred in 1752. In that year Great Britain gave up the old Julian calendar of Julius Caesar and joined most of Western Europe in adopting the Gregorian calendar of 1582. To reconcile the differences between the two calendars, it was agreed that ten days should be added to the dates of events that occurred before 1700—thus we say that the Mayflower Compact was signed November 21, although the document is dated November 11. And eleven days were added to the dates of events between 1700 and 1752. In this book we've adapted pre-1752 dates to the modern style whenever we established that our source was based on the old calendar.

Index

References to illustrations are printed in boldface.

Stephens, Ann Sophia, 6/9
Steuben, Baron von, 2/23
Stevens, John L, 1/17, 2/6
Stewart, A. T., 9/21
Stieglitz, Alfred, 11/24
Stilwell, Gen. Joseph, 1/28
Stone, Lucy, 9/6
Stowe, Harriet Beecher, 3/20, 8/21
Straus, Oscar S., 10/23
Strauss, Levi, 5/20
Streetcars, 11/26
Strong, George Templeton, 1/21, 3/27, 4/25, 5/9, 5/14, 10/19, 12/31
Stuart, Gilbert, 5/6, 8/24
Stuyvesant, Peter, **5/27**
Subway system (N.Y.), 10/27
Suffrage, 2/8, 2/27, 3/23, 5/1, 7/2, 7/19, 7/28, 8/1, 8/26, 9/6, 11/5
Sullivan, John L., 7/8, 9/7
Sullivan, Louis, **12/9**
Sumner, Charles, 5/22
Supermarkets, 10/9
Supreme Court, 9/15, 9/21, 9/26, 12/3
Sutter, John, **1/24**
Syracuse University, 1/23

Taft, William Howard, 9/15
Talbot, George, 10/31
Tammany Hall, 5/12, 12/4
Tariffs, 4/11, 11/24
Taxation, 6/9, 7/12, 8/2
Taylor, Zachary, 1/7, 11/24
Teamsters Union, 7/30
Teapot Dome scandal, 4/7

Tecumseh, 8/12
Telegraph, 4/3, 5/24, **7/27**, 8/16, 10/24, 11/6
Telephone, 1/28, **3/10**, 8/4, **8/30**, 9/24
Television, **1/25**, 4/7, 4/30, 5/11, 10/11
Temperance movement, 5/24, 6/2, 9/6
Tennessee, 1/26, 6/1, 8/23
Tennessee Valley Authority (TVA), 5/18
Tennis, 8/31
Terry, Luther, 1/12
Texas, 1/5, 1/10, 1/17, 2/24, 3/6, 3/10, 4/5, 4/21, 8/25, 9/1, 12/29
Thanksgiving Day, 11/26
Theater, 4/16, 11/25, 12/27, 12/30
Theosophical Society, 11/17
Thomas, Parnell, 5/26
Thoreau, Henry David, **7/23**
Three Mile Island, 3/28
Thurmond, Strom, 7/17
Tilden, Samuel J., 11/7
Time zones, 11/18
Titanic (boat), **4/14**
Tobacco, 5/3, 6/29
"Tokyo Rose," 1/19
Tomb of the Unknown Soldier, 11/11
Towner, Rev. Margaret, 5/23
Townes, Charles H., 3/22
Townsend Plan, 7/16
Townshend Revenue Acts, 6/29
Traffic light, 8/5
Treasury Department, 9/2
Trenton, Battle of, 12/26
Triangle fire, **3//25**

Tripoli pirates, 2/16, 9/5
Truman, Harry S, 3/22, 4/11, 5/8, 7/1, 7/22, 7/26, 10/25, **11/3**, 11/9
Truth-in-Packaging, 11/3
Turkey, wild, 1/26, **5/17**
Turner, Nat, 8/22
Tuskegee Institute, 12/30
Tweed, William Marcy "Boss," **12/4**
Twentieth Century Limited (train), 6/8
Tyler, John, 3/29
Tyler, Royall, 4/16
Typewriter, **6/23**

Un-American Activities, House Committee on, 5/26, 10/20
Uncle Tom's Cabin (Stowe), **3/20**
Underground Railroad, 2/19
Union Pacific Railroad, 3/2
United Mine Workers (UMW), 4/1, 9/11
United Nations, 6/26, 8/21, 10/4
United States (name adopted), 9/9
U.S. Steel Corporation, 2/25
Utah, 1/4, 3/10, 8/1
Utopian communities, **1/3, 6/1,** 6/5

Vacuum cleaner, **6/8**
Valley Forge, 12/17
Vanderbilt, Alva (Mrs. William K.), **3/26**
Vanderbilt, George, 12/6